HOW DOES THE SHOW GO ON?

THOMAS SCHUMACHER *with* JEFF KURTTI

EDITIONS

NEW YORK

HOW DOES THE SHOW GO ON?

an INTRODUCTION TO THE THEATER

by THOMAS SCHUMACHER Producer of the Tony Award®-Winning
Broadway Musical *The Lion King*

with JEFF KURTTI

For information, address Disney Editions, 114 Fifth Avenue, New York, New York 10011-5690.

Disney Editions
Editorial Director: Wendy Lefkon
Senior Editor: Jody Revenson
Assistant Editor: Jessica Ward

How Does the Show Go On? is produced by becker&mayer!, Bellevue, Washington
www.beckermayer.com

Design: Kasey Free
Editorial: Jenna Free, Meghan Cleary, and Amy Wideman
Production Management: Leah Finger and Diane Ross
Illustrations (pages 7, 16–17, and 124): Scott Tilley

Library of Congress Cataloging-in-Publication data on file.

ISBN 978-1-4231-2031-5
10 9 8 7 6 5 4 3 2 1

Second Edition/First Printing

This edition has been updated to include new Disney on Broadway show material.

Visit disneybooks.com

Printed in China

This is me in Summer Repertory Theatre's summer stock production of South Pacific.

Here I am at sixteen years old playing Barnaby Tucker in San Mateo Community Theatre's production of Hello Dolly. I was never much of a jumper.

Disney Theatrical Group

Dear Reader,

I don't remember ever not loving stories told from a stage. When I was a kid, my mom would play albums from old musicals on the family stereo, and the stories would play out in my mind.

"Theater" is a pretty big word. It means a lot of things to a lot of people. To me, it has always meant a place where everything is possible.

Theater has many purposes. First, it is about creating a show for the audience. Of course, to do that you need a story written by a playwright, actors to perform it, a director and designers to put it onstage, and—sometimes—composers and lyricists to write the songs.

It is a business, it is a hobby, it is a place to go to work, a place to play with your friends, a place to learn about yourself, and a place to learn about others. Theater can take place at school, in your garage, in a big fancy building, or even outside in the open air.

For me, the theater is a family. I grew up in rehearsal rooms and in dark theaters, sitting among anxious audiences, and backstage with a view of all the magic from behind the scenes. The theater is home for me, and I'd like to invite you in to take a look at what we do. Maybe you'll want to join the family, too.

It is my hope that within these pages you will find something you didn't know, something you didn't know you didn't know, and something that you'll want to know more about.

So let's begin with what seems like a simple question: "How Does the Show Go On?"

Table of Contents

ACT TWO

ENCORE

OVERTURE What Should You Know First?

What's Theater?

A theater is any space where performances take place. Plays, dance concerts, and operas all happen in theaters. A theater can be a formal building downtown or a platform in your garage or church basement. Lots of schools have theaters (sometimes these are called auditoriums) and most towns have some sort of theater building.

More than just a building, though, the word "theater" refers to everything connected with the theatrical arts—the play itself, along with the stage, scenery, lighting, makeup, costumes, music, dancing, acting, and actors. For example, when someone says, "I work in the theater," they might mean they actually work in a specific building, or they might mean they contribute somehow to producing a show. Or they are just being snooty.

Even when there is no audience in a theater, it is a busy place with things like rehearsals and makeup application going on backstage.

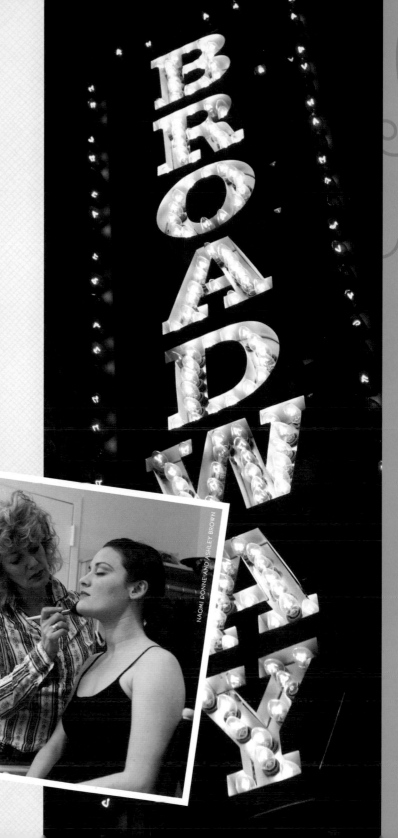

NAOMI DONNE AND ASHLEY BROWN

11

BROADWAY

Kinds of Shows

BROADWAY AND OFF-BROADWAY

In New York City, there are two main types of live theater: Broadway and Off-Broadway. The term **Broadway** comes from the legendary street of the same name, and a "Broadway show" is a play or musical performed in one of the specially designated theaters along or very near this street. The word can also refer to a traveling show that has once been in one of these theaters; your town may have a "Broadway Series" featuring these usually famous plays that have been performed on Broadway.

    Off-Broadway means a couple of things. In New York, theaters that are smaller than a Broadway theater are called "Off-Broadway" theaters. Often, these theaters show different kinds of plays or musicals that work better in small settings, either because of the show's topic or because they draw smaller audiences.

    The longest-running play in the history of New York, *The Fantasticks*, played Off-Broadway for 42 years!

Mary Poppins *plays here at* Broadway's New Amsterdam Theatre.

THE WEST END

In London, Broadway-style shows are called **West End** shows because they are performed in the West End of London. After a while, when people see enough shows of a similar style in one neighborhood, they begin to describe the plays by that location. So depending on where you are, you might call the same type of play a "Broadway show" or a "West End show."

The Lion King *plays in* London's Lyceum Theatre in the "West End."

TOURING SHOWS

A show that is successful and popular in New York or London is often restaged around the country and around the world. Sometimes these are productions that load into trucks so that the show can be seen in cities all over the United States on what is called a **domestic tour**. The entire production can also be loaded into boats or on airplanes to be seen all over the world. These **international tours** have made Broadway famous all over the globe. Putting these on *can* be tricky because the sets have to look big and Broadway-style, but they also need to be packed up and transported between theaters. The actors as well as much of the stage crew and orchestra also have to travel from city to city. Foreign productions need new casts and often require translations. You can hear *The Lion King* performed onstage in English, Dutch, German, Korean, Japanese, and French!

PHILADELPHIA PREMIERE!

Disney PRESENTS

THE LION KING

BROADWAY'S AWARD-WINNING BEST MUSICAL

JUNE 8–SEPTEMBER 10
ACADEMY OF MUSIC

The Lion King *in Shanghai, China*

DID YOU KNOW?

The Lion King has been seen all over the world. When it went to Shanghai, China, on tour, we put the sets and costumes on a plane from Australia, where the show had just been performed. The same set was then loaded onto a boat and sailed to South Africa for performances there.

THE MARK TAPER FORUM

A regional theater, a summer stock theater, and my hometown's community theater (top to bottom). I worked at all these places.

SRT
summer repertory theatre

San Mateo Performing Arts Center

BROADWAY BY THE BAY

REGIONAL THEATERS

Regional theaters (sometimes called resident theaters) are professional theater companies located in cities throughout the United States. These theaters are very important, because they present both new plays that have never been seen anywhere else, and classic plays that may have been written more than a hundred years ago. Over the course of time, local audiences that see many plays in the same space often form a relationship with both the actors and the people who put on the shows there.

Some people like to "subscribe" to their local theater. In the same way that a newspaper or magazine subscription comes to your house on a regular basis, a theater subscription buys you tickets for a number of plays so that you can keep going to the theater again and again.

SUMMER STOCK

Summer stock theaters are a long tradition in America. A combination of professional, early professional, and student actors gather, primarily in resort areas, to put on classic, or "stock," plays for the local and tourist audiences during the summer months. Many of the greatest actors in the theater today got their start in summer stock productions.

Many people in theater have romantic notions about being in summer stock productions because the plays are put together very quickly with limited rehearsal time. Everyone works what seems like twenty-four hours a day to get the show on. Sometimes surprises happen right up until show time; at the very last minute of rehearsal, a star from television or Broadway might come in and play the lead!

The thrill for the audience is not only being able to see great performances of classic plays, but also to know that there is an extraordinary burst of energy in every show.

COMMUNITY THEATERS

For people who love the theater, few things are as much fun as gathering with friends to put on a play. In **community theater**, most or all of the participants are unpaid, or "amateurs," which is why community theater is also called amateur theater. While some people's parents spend the weekend gardening or playing golf, others spend the weekend performing for an audience.

Styles of Theaters

Just like there are lots of types of shows, there are many different kinds of theaters. The main thing that makes them different is where the audience sits in relation to the stage—and there are several options.

PROSCENIUM

Probably the most familiar kind, a **proscenium** theater is where the action of the show takes place on a stage at the front of the room, and the audience sits facing the stage. A big arch, or "proscenium," oftentimes with a curtain, separates the audience from the stage area. Proscenium stages range in size from very big to very small.

THRUST STAGE

A **thrust stage** is like a proscenium, but with an additional piece. The "thrust" is an extra section of the stage area that extends beyond the proscenium into the audience. The thrust stage can be anything from a small extension to almost a full stage in and of itself, but in all cases the audience surrounds it on three sides.

AMPHITHEATER

The **amphitheater** is one of the oldest kinds of formal theaters. Ancient Greeks and Romans both used amphitheaters. In those days, a classical amphitheater was built outdoors, with a semicircular seating section raised up to look down on to the stage. The Romans created amphitheaters this way because their bowl shapes hold sound very well (and microphones would not be invented until almost two thousand years later!).

DID YOU KNOW?

The largest amphitheater in North America, in Devore, California, seats 65,000 people! Most amphitheaters are much smaller than that.

Notice how close the audience sits to this thrust stage.

15

These days, an amphitheater is good for music as well as plays that don't require lots of scenery. Most modern-day theaters are still shaped to naturally amplify the actors' voices, so it's often unnecessary for anyone to use a microphone.

THEATER-IN-THE-ROUND

Any theater where the audience is seated on all sides of the stage is known as a **theater-in-the-round**. The stage itself can be round, square, triangular, or any closed shape, with actors entering and exiting through the audience from different directions or from under the stage. The stage is usually on the same level with, or near the height of, the front row.

Of course, having the audience on all sides can be a problem, since the actors always have their backs facing some part of the audience. However, in-the-round theater allows more people to sit close to the action.

BLACK-BOX

A **black-box** theater is a space where no permanent stage or seating area is built-in. The stage and the audience can be set up in-the-round, thrust, or proscenium style, depending on what the director wants. This kind of theater gives complete control to each director and designer, allowing them to decide what setup will best tell their story. This flexible theater style became popular towards the end of the 20th century. Black-box theaters can also be built inside existing buildings, such as warehouses, or even in your own garage at home.

DESIGNING YOUR THEATER

Here's a fun way to try out how different theaters work. Take a playing card (the ace of spades is always a good choice) and 200 jelly beans. The card is the stage, and the beans are the people. How many ways can you organize the beans so that they can see the stage? If you put the beans in rows all on one side, the beans in the back rows are far from the card. If you put the beans in circular rows around the card, many more of the beans are close to the card. In the same way, directors must decide what kind of theater works best for their play: proscenium, thrust, or in-the-round.

black-box

amphitheater

proscenium

thrust stage

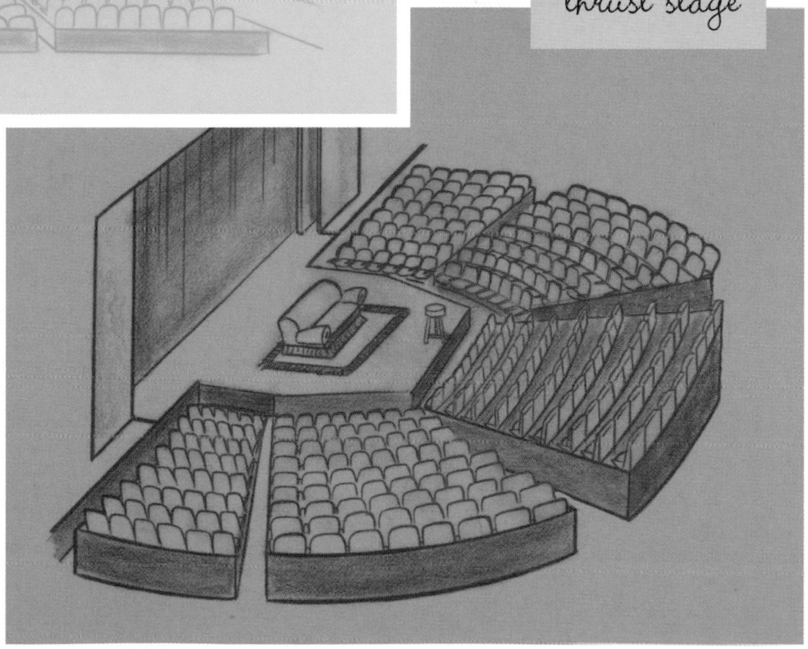

ACT ONE

Front of House: From the Street to the Stage Apron

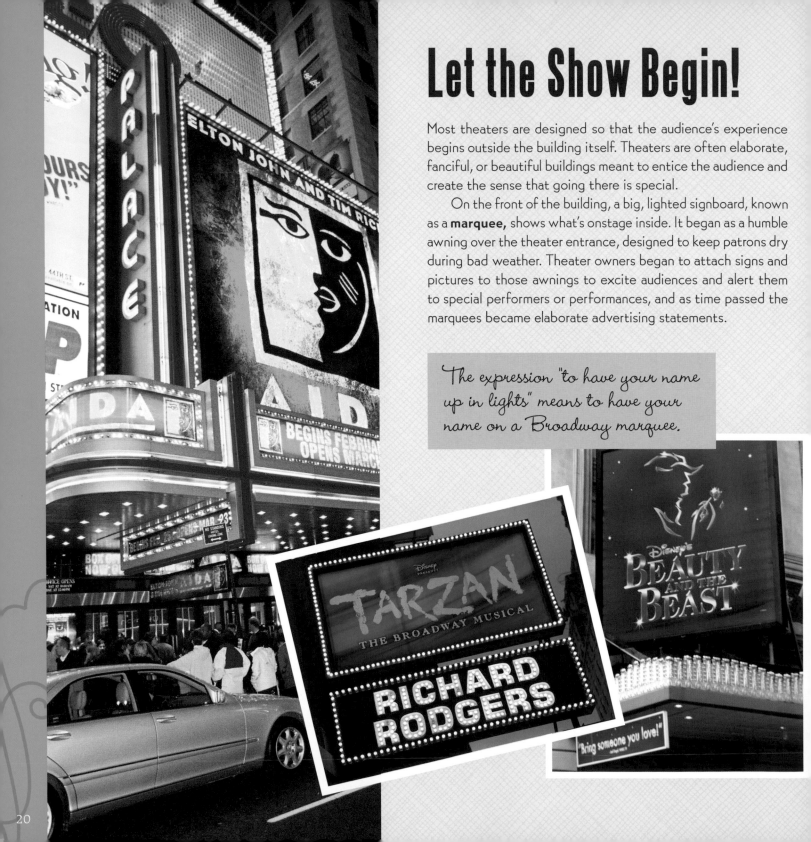

Let the Show Begin!

Most theaters are designed so that the audience's experience begins outside the building itself. Theaters are often elaborate, fanciful, or beautiful buildings meant to entice the audience and create the sense that going there is special.

On the front of the building, a big, lighted signboard, known as a **marquee,** shows what's onstage inside. It began as a humble awning over the theater entrance, designed to keep patrons dry during bad weather. Theater owners began to attach signs and pictures to those awnings to excite audiences and alert them to special performers or performances, and as time passed the marquees became elaborate advertising statements.

The expression "to have your name up in lights" means to have your name on a Broadway marquee.

WHAT'S A BOX OFFICE?

Inside the doors of the theater building, you'll find a window, booth, or other area where tickets are sold called the **box office**. No one is really sure why it's called that, but people in the theater like to make up stories: here are two. Some people say it's called the box office because historically, people may have gone there to arrange to sit in a "box," which was a special area containing several seats usually set aside for people who want to *be seen* more than they want to see the play. Other people believe that the name comes from when admission to the theater only cost a single coin, which was dropped into a little slot on the top of a small, locked box. However the term came into use, today's box office is where people buy tickets or pick up tickets they've paid for in advance.

In the box office, the **treasurer** (no, not somebody hoarding a big box of jewels!) is in charge of guarding the tickets and the money paid for them, and for selling tickets to people who want to see the show.

The term "box office" can also refer to the total sales from a performance. You might ask, "How was tonight's box office?" That doesn't mean you want to know if it was cold in there or if they had fun. You are simply asking if they made much money that night.

When a show takes in more money in a given week at a theater than any show before it, the show is said to have set a **box-office record**. When *Tarzan* opened at the Richard Rodgers Theatre on Broadway, it set that theater's all-time sales records for several weeks in a row!

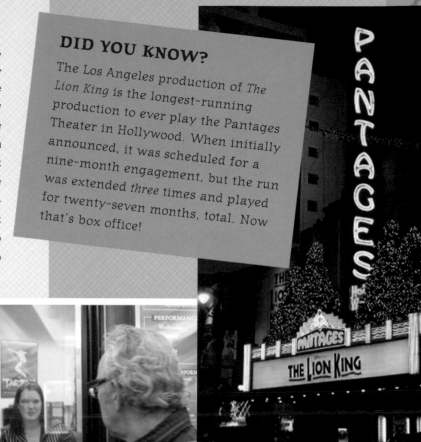

DID YOU KNOW?

The Los Angeles production of *The Lion King* is the longest-running production to ever play the Pantages Theater in Hollywood. When initially announced, it was scheduled for a nine-month engagement, but the run was extended *three* times and played for twenty-seven months, total. Now that's box office!

Traditional Broadway shows perform eight times a week, but you need to check the box office for dates and times.

Disney PRESENTS

THE LION KING

BROADWAY'S AWARD-WINNING BEST MUSICAL

PERFORMANCE SCHEDULE
NOW THROUGH SEPTEMBER 3, 2006

TUESDAY	8 PM
WEDNESDAY	2 & 8 PM
THURSDAY	8 PM
FRIDAY	8 PM
SATURDAY	2 & 8 PM
SUNDAY	3 PM

THAT'S THE TICKET

At its simplest, a **ticket** is a paper receipt that proves that you have paid your admission to a play, a movie, the zoo, a museum, or even Disneyland. Theater tickets contain information such as the name of the show, the date of the performance, and often the specific place you are going to sit. Sometimes tickets are sold for *any* available seat, which is called "general admission," as opposed to "reserved seating," which buys you an assigned seat.

Theater tickets used to all look alike, but now they come in many different sizes. Some tickets can be printed from your home computer; those tickets have a barcode on them that ticket takers scan at the door when they let you in.

WHO'S WILL, AND WHY SHOULD HE CALL?

When you order theater tickets over the phone or on the Internet you'll find them at the box office at a special window called **will call**. This name is short for "the place where we hope

HOW TO READ A TICKET

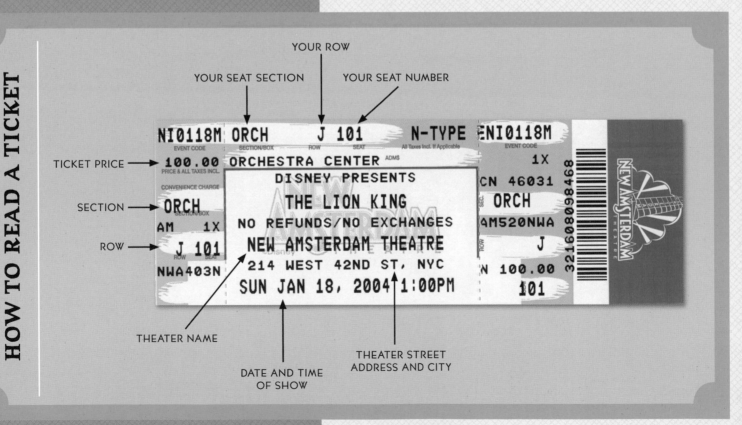

YOUR SHOW TICKET IS ENCLOSED

you *will* come and *call* your name so we know which tickets are yours." They usually want the person who ordered the tickets to bring their order-confirmation number, the credit card they used to buy the tickets, and a photo ID. That's to keep people from getting someone else's tickets by mistake. Ticket mix-ups can be a real mess. Sometimes tickets for the same seat are accidentally duplicated and four people are trying to sit in the same seat. Other times, latecomers arrive only to find that the show has started and someone is sitting in the seats they paid a lot of money for. These mix-ups can cause a major disruption or delay of the show. Sometimes they become the show themselves. Just recently, the police had to be called to a major Broadway hit because audience members began fighting over who was the real owner of the tickets!

I'VE GOT MY TICKET, BUT WHERE AM I GOING?
Ticket takers, who are stationed at entry doors to the auditorium, are responsible for checking your ticket; they sometimes tear the ticket and give back the "stub," which many people keep as a souvenir.

LOBBY

Once the ticket taker has checked your ticket, you'll pass through the theater **lobby** on your way to the auditorium. The lobby is a large gathering area where people can meet their friends, stand and visit with each other, find the restrooms (a *great* idea before every show—moms are right about that!), and often buy drinks, snacks, and souvenirs. Lobbies are also fun places to watch for interesting people. You might see some crazy types—and the crazier the show, the crazier the audience! That's part of the fun.

MAKING MEMORIES

In the lobby, you can shop for souvenirs at the merchandise counter. One of the most popular items you can buy is a **souvenir program**, which is a large, collectible book that has many photographs of the production.

Big theaters often have tons of stuff at their merchandise counters, like T-shirts, mugs, dolls, and, of course, souvenir programs, to remind visitors of the show they've seen. Selling all these things is also a good way for the theater to get rich.

Souvenir books have great photos of the show you are seeing.

HOUSELIGHTS BLINK

One of the ways you know it is time to take your seat is that the lights in the lobby will blink. This is a time-honored code that means, "we are ready to start." Another method of alerting the audience is the playing of chimes—sort of like a clock sounding. These two methods can be used before the show or at the end of intermission. If you see blinking lights or hear chimes, get back to your seat. You don't want to miss anything.

HOUSE MANAGER

The person in charge of getting everyone in the door and settled into the theater is called the **house manager**.

House managers oversee the ushers and ticket takers, and are responsible for making sure that everyone finds their seats in time for the start of the show. **Ushers** are the people who greet you at the door to the auditorium and escort you to your seat. The usher will also provide a **program** that has information about the show, its cast, and creators. (Programs are also good for fanning yourself if the theater is too warm!)

The house manager is also in charge of ensuring the audience's comfort and safety. The house manager uses a phone or radio headset that's sort of like a walkie-talkie to reach the stage manager backstage. A show never starts until the house manager says it's okay.

House managers are very important. Their staff is the first experience most audiences have with a show, and the better that experience, the better the rest of the show will be. "You only get one chance to make a first impression" is the rule for all good house managers. The best house managers are really good at dealing with nutty people who like to talk or take pictures during the show.

The house manager (right center) keeps everyone moving to his or her seat and is in contact with everyone backstage.

BOX SEATS

ORCHESTRA PIT

AISLE

ROW

In the House

AUDITORIUM

Once you leave the lobby and go into the seating area, you will have entered the **auditorium**. Many theater people also call this "the house." A classic expression is "the house is open," meaning that the ushers have begun seating people. Actors and technicians always want to know when the house is open so that they don't just walk out onstage or make unnecessary noise. When the house is open, the show is about to begin, so no one wants to see an actor who is in costume but not "in character" just pop out from behind the curtain.

The auditorium is basically a big room—often wonderfully decorated—where the audience sits and watches the show. Depending on how large the theater is, the auditorium may be divided up into different areas, and sometimes different levels. There are many names for these areas, and they differ around the world.

Aisles: The passageway between or alongside the seats in the auditorium is called the **aisle**. Similar walking paths in a church or an airplane are also called aisles, as are the spaces between the displays in a department store or supermarket.

Rows: Seats are all arranged facing the stage, usually in **rows**. Each seat in a row is numbered so you can locate where you're supposed to sit by the row letter and seat number. For example, your seat might be "Row F, Seat 104." This system helps people find the seats that they reserved when they bought their ticket.

The seating area is often sloped toward the stage (this slope is called a "rake") to offer good views of the stage from every seat. Otherwise, you might just see the back of the head of the guy in front of you. And if you end up looking at the back of someone's hat, tell him: "I paid for a ticket, too!"

There's not just ONE great seat in a theater, and any seat is always better than NO seat!

The Best Seat in the House?: Many people can't decide where the best place to sit is—and it is a very good question. There are many things to consider. The price of the ticket is higher for the best view of the stage. Some people like to sit higher up to see the entire "stage picture," particularly to view the staging and choreography. Others like to sit very near the stage just to see the actors' faces close up.

I like to see shows often, and I've sat in seats all over the theater. My rule of thumb is to try sitting in several locations over time. You'll get a sense of where you want to be. The most important rule is to never sit where people think you are "supposed" to sit, just because it is expensive. Sit wherever you can get a seat and enjoy the play.

Downstairs: Generally in America the main floor is called the **orchestra** section. (In Ancient Greece, the "orchestra" was the space between the seating area and the stage, where the chorus and the instrumentalists sat. This is how the modern orchestra got its name.) In London, this area is called the *stalls* (in Shakespeare's time the main floor was not the best seating; in fact they didn't sit at all—they stood just like horses in a "stall").

Upstairs: The second level has many names. Sometimes it is called the **mezzanine**, sometimes the **balcony**. In London, it is called the **dress circle** or the **upper circle**. It can be very confusing, but there is always signage to tell you where to go, and your ticket always says what section you are to sit in.

Box Seats: Along the sides of the auditorium, there are often very fancy little seating areas for small groups, set aside in private "balconies" facing toward the audience and stage. These are called **box seats**, and although they look very cool, they are *not* a place to sit when you want an especially good view of the action on stage—they're more for when you want to *be seen yourself*!

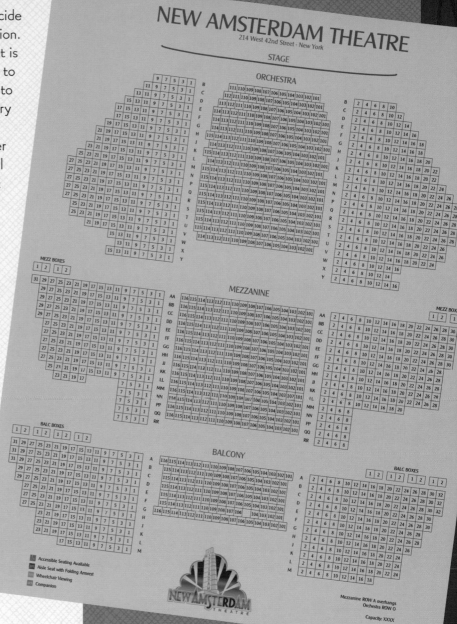

The seating chart shows exactly where every seat is. At the box office you can look at the chart and decide which seat is best for you.

SITTING PRETTY

A **program** is a flyer, booklet, or magazine listing of the order of events and other important information, including a cast list, cast photos, cast biographies, song lists with singers' names (if it's a musical show), and a list of scenes.

The usher will usually give you a program on the way to your seat. One of the best parts of going to a show is sitting down with a fresh program and learning a little bit about what is going to happen and who is going to be performing.

Programs also make great souvenirs from the show. Some theaters have very elaborate programs with essays on the play's topic. These are fun to read after you go home.

Sometimes when you go to a show you get a **Playbill**. Playbill is the most famous publisher of theater programs in America, and their logo is a symbol of Broadway theater. The founder of the company, Mr. Strauss, thought of giving a program to the audience with information about the show and selling advertising in it like it was a little magazine. This was a very smart idea, and is great for the audience because it gives them important information for free.

One of the best theater collections you can start is a collection of programs from the shows you've seen. Start collecting programs now and in a few years you'll look back and remember the shows you saw just like you were there again. I collected all the Playbills from my first trip to New York when I was in college, and those programs still remind me of the very first night I sat down in a Broadway theater. They sit in a box with programs going back to the first big show I performed in when I was in the 4th grade!

Sometimes box seats have terrible views of the show, but great views of backstage. I love sitting there the second time I see a show, so I can see how they do it. Stagehands aren't always interesting to look at, so I recommend seeing the show *first* and then looking into "the wings."

Standing Room: Many theaters have special floor space where they can sell tickets for people to stand, usually when all the seats are filled, known as **standing room**.

You might hear a *very* popular show described as "standing room only" (abbreviated as SRO), which means that it is so well-attended that all of the seats are taken, leaving only the standing areas. It is tiring to stand all night, but worth it if the ticket is really cheap and the show is really good!

I don't recommend it for long operas. I learned that the hard way.

SETTLING IN

Once you have found your seat, it's always fun to look around the theater and see how it is decorated, or just watch the other people in the audience arrive and find their seats. Notice how many people still dress in their best clothing to attend the the-ater, which is a long-standing tradition, and still a fun part of the show, especially on Broadway.

As you look around the theater, you might notice certain things right away. The **proscenium arch**, for example, is the "frame" that separates the stage from the audience, through which the action of a play is viewed.

You'll probably notice a ledge between the curtain and the orchestra pit in front of the curtain. This is the edge of the stage, and is called the **stage apron**, or just the apron. In some theaters, a mechanical lift can raise the floor of the orchestra pit to the same level as the stage, extending the stage apron further into the audience.

An **orchestra pit** is the area in front of the orchestra-level seats, and it's just what it sounds like: a big hole in the floor where the orchestra or band plays live music to accompany the performance.

The conductor stands in the pit, and you can usually see his head popping up as he directs the music. If there is no live music, this area is usually covered with a platform to add more seats.

Beautiful box seats (above) and the orchestra pit (below)

DID YOU KNOW...

One of the most dangerous things in the theater is the possibility of falling off the stage into the orchestra pit. Everyone who has worked in the theater for a long time has seen this happen. There are many safety rules about "the pit" and for a good reason—it can be a very long way down!

Take a look at this page of the script from Tarzan®. . . .

Who's Who?

PLAYWRIGHT

You'd think that a person who writes plays wou
play**write**. But actually, it's spelled play**wright**,
coincidence that the words sound the same

Plays are actually said to be "wrough
wrought-iron railing or wrought-iron piece
when something is "wrought" it is heated, h
bent into shape. The title "playwright" sugg
are hard, physical work created by craftsm
means that playwrights want a name that i
like everyone else who works in the theater.

Writing plays is a particular form of writ
ists write articles for magazines or newspaper
what has happened or their opinions about ever
write stories in the form of a book, and poets
to be read alone or in collections. The **playw**
the story and the dialogue of a play, as well as
stage directions that the actors and director fo
story for the stage. Writing a play is a bit like wr
because the writer must create characters and p
like writing music because you don't *really* kno
have written until you hear it performed and l
it sounds out loud.

In *Tarzan*, playwright David Henry Hwang cre
dialogue and actions for the characters to perfo
rectors follow these "stage directions" very clo
ten. Other directors just ignore them complete
them fight about that later.) Sometimes when you
the stage directions come from the original pro
are specific to the original scenery and cast. You
make up new staging and don't need to follow v
ten—though usually the people who wrote it are
and have a good idea of how you might think abo

Take a look at this page of the script from Tarzan®. . . .

Who's Who?

PLAYWRIGHT

You'd think that a person who writes plays would be called a play**write**. But actually, it's spelled play**wright**, and it's just a coincidence that the words sound the same.

Plays are actually said to be "wrought," just like a wrought-iron railing or wrought-iron piece of furniture; when something is "wrought" it is heated, hammered, and bent into shape. The title "playwright" suggests that plays are hard, physical work created by craftsmen. Or it just means that playwrights want a name that is special, just like everyone else who works in the theater.

Writing plays is a particular form of writing. Journalists write articles for magazines or newspapers, and report what has happened or their opinions about events. Novelists write stories in the form of a book, and poets write poems to be read alone or in collections. The **playwright** writes the story and the dialogue of a play, as well as many of the stage directions that the actors and director follow, to tell a story for the stage. Writing a play is a bit like writing a novel, because the writer must create characters and plot. It is also like writing music because you don't *really* know what you have written until you hear it performed and listen to how it sounds out loud.

In *Tarzan*, playwright David Henry Hwang created specific dialogue and actions for the characters to perform. Some directors follow these "stage directions" very closely as written. Other directors just ignore them completely. (Let's let them fight about that later.) Sometimes when you read a play, the stage directions come from the original production and are specific to the original scenery and cast. You can always make up new staging and don't need to follow what is written—though usually the people who wrote it are pretty smart and have a good idea of how you might think about it.

Sometimes box seats have terrible views of the show, but great views of backstage. I love sitting there the second time I see a show, so I can see how they do it. Stagehands aren't always interesting to look at, so I recommend seeing the show *first* and then looking into "the wings."

Standing Room: Many theaters have special floor space where they can sell tickets for people to stand, usually when all the seats are filled, known as **standing room**.

You might hear a *very* popular show described as "standing room only" (abbreviated as SRO), which means that it is so well-attended that all of the seats are taken, leaving only the standing areas. It is tiring to stand all night, but worth it if the ticket is really cheap and the show is really good!

I don't recommend it for long operas. I learned that the hard way.

SETTLING IN

Once you have found your seat, it's always fun to look around the theater and see how it is decorated, or just watch the other people in the audience arrive and find their seats. Notice how many people still dress in their best clothing to attend the theater, which is a long-standing tradition, and still a fun part of the show, especially on Broadway.

As you look around the theater, you might notice certain things right away. The **proscenium arch**, for example, is the "frame" that separates the stage from the audience, through which the action of a play is viewed.

You'll probably notice a ledge between the curtain and the orchestra pit in front of the curtain. This is the edge of the stage, and is called the **stage apron**, or just the apron. In some theaters, a mechanical lift can raise the floor of the orchestra pit to the same level as the stage, extending the stage apron further into the audience.

An **orchestra pit** is the area in front of the orchestra-level seats, and it's just what it sounds like: a big hole in the floor where the orchestra or band plays live music to accompany the performance.

The conductor stands in the pit, and you can usually see his head popping up as he directs the music. If there is no live music, this area is usually covered with a platform to add more seats.

Beautiful box seats (above) and the orchestra pit (below)

DID YOU KNOW...

One of the most dangerous things in the theater is the possibility of falling off the stage into the orchestra pit. Everyone who has worked in the theater for a long time has seen this happen. There are many safety rules about "the pit" and for a good reason—it can be a very long way down!

29

Stage Notes

★ David Henry Hwang does his best writing lying down, in longhand, on legal-size pads of paper. Only later does he type out the script using a computer. For *Tarzan*, we got him a special yoga mat, so he could write new dialogue and scenes during rehearsal!

★ Playwrights often say that scenes aren't written, they are rewritten, because actors and directors ask for so many changes. Playwrights have to fight very hard to keep actors from changing the lines without permission, or from simply learning them incorrectly.

★ Julian Fellowes, who wrote "the book" for *Mary Poppins*, began his career as an actor. When he writes dialogue he always thinks about how it would sound coming out of an actor and not how it looks on the page. Maybe that's why he won an Oscar for writing the film *Gosford Park*.

★ Roger Allers co-directed the animated version of *The Lion King*, and Irene Mecchi co-wrote its screenplay, so they were the perfect team to write the book for the stage musical.

Tarzan® playwright David Henry Hwang reviews important script changes with associate director Jeff Lee.

TRY YOUR HAND AT WRITING:

Playwrights have to put down on paper the way different people sound when they talk. This is called writing in a particular "voice." See if you can write a one-page scene between three people you know. Be sure to include some stage directions to capture their personalities. Don't use their real names, but show it to them and see if they can guess who is who.

Was your selection of words specific to the way they speak in real life? Did it capture their personalities? Did it surprise them that you were able to capture their attitude by writing in the way that they speak?

Director Sir Richard Eyre with Mary Poppins book writer Julian Fellowes

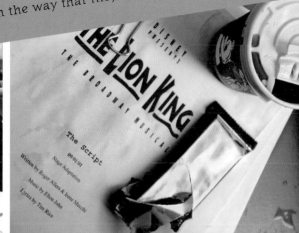

Julie Taymor, backstage at The Lion King

Director Robert Longbottom reviews changes with associate director Tom Kosis for On the Record.

The Little Mermaid director Francesca Zambello and choreographer Stephen Mear watch over every detail.

DIRECTOR

"Hey! Who's in charge here?" That question gets asked a lot in life, but inside a theater everyone knows it is the director who is in charge.

There are all sorts of "directors" in life, and they are usually some type of boss. They may be the director of sales at a department store, or on the board of directors at the local symphony or museum.

Directors are always in charge of something. In the theater, the **director** is in charge of everything that happens onstage. They don't act—the actors do that—and they don't design the sets, costumes, or lights—the designers do that—but the directors guide the cast and crew toward the goal of creating a wonderful production.

The best directors hire the best people, and they all work together to create a show that feels like it is all one person's idea, or *vision*. Some directors can also act, design, produce, or write—but every great director knows that when they are directing they need to focus on the show as a whole.

Stage Notes

★ In 1998, Julie Taymor was the first woman to ever win a Tony Award for directing a musical—*The Lion King*—on Broadway. That was seventy-eight years after women won the right to vote! What took so long?

★ The best directors have a deep knowledge of every part of stagecraft, including scenery, lighting, and costumes—not just acting. Some directors are loud and bossy, and there is no mistaking who they are. Others almost whisper. The job is to get the show on the stage and there are many ways of doing it. One legendary director I've worked with won't let actors stand up and begin staging the show until they have memorized all their lines. He won't let anyone hold a script in rehearsal. Frankly, I thought he was nutty.

★ Julie Taymor has studied theater techniques and directed shows all over the world. Her staging and designs for *The Lion King* don't just mirror Africa, but weave together scenes from America, Europe, Asia, and Africa.

★ Robert Jess Roth, who directed the original stage production of *Beauty and the Beast*, had the idea of putting the animated film on Broadway before anyone at Disney thought about doing Broadway shows. That one idea started the entire Disney-on-Broadway business.

★ Julie Taymor had never seen the film of *The Lion King* before she was asked to direct it on Broadway.

★ Sir Richard Eyre, who directed *Mary Poppins* and ran the National Theater of Britain for ten years, was knighted by the Queen of England in 1996.

Director Richard Eyre spends a private moment with Mary Poppins herself, Ashley Brown.

COMPOSER

Some straight plays have music that is played under the action or between the scenes, but all musicals are built around the work of the **composer**. Some of the most popular music of the twentieth century was written for musicals—often the songs become better known than the shows they were written for!

Perhaps the single most important choice for a musical is who the composer will be. It may be even more important than the idea, because even some pretty goofy ideas can turn into successful musicals if the songs are memorable.

Composers write many different styles of music for the theater. They can write rock music like Phil Collins did for *Tarzan*, they can write traditional musical songs like the popular ones Alan Menken wrote for *Beauty and the Beast*, or they can write in what's called "World Music"—a specific ethnic style like Lebo M used for *The Lion King*, incorporating beautiful African chants and songs. Some composers are great musical performers, and others can barely play an instrument. One famous Broadway composer could only hum his songs, so he sat next to someone at the piano while they figured out the notes and the chords to create the music.

The music in a show can tell you where you are, how the characters feel, and what the overall mood is. The composer of a musical is also responsible for the music played between the scenes and during dance numbers. The composer often has a musical staff to help with all of these assignments.

Phil Collins is a famous singer and drummer, but he wrote all the music and lyrics for Tarzan®.

"We are the music makers, and we are the dreamers of dreams."

Arthur O'Shaughnessy, "Ode"

Alan Menken has eight Academy Awards®, but it is the Broadway sound that makes his songs so special.

Stage Notes

* Eight songs were added to the Oscar-winning score of *Beauty and the Beast* in its transition from animated feature film to Broadway. Seven of those songs were written by Alan Menken and Sir Tim Rice.

* There's a musical number in the stage version of *Beauty and the Beast* called "Human Again," sung by a group of characters that have been turned into household objects by a curse, where they dream of being turned back into humans. The song was originally written for the film but ultimately wasn't included. After the song became popular onstage, the film's original directors and producer completed the abandoned animated sequence for the film's re-release on IMAX and DVD.

* International superstar Phil Collins, who wrote the music for *Tarzan*, grew so attached to the Broadway production that he bought an apartment in New York just so he could be closer to the show. He continued to watch it a few nights a week and was an integral part of the production at all points from script development to casting to staging.

* One of the most beautiful songs in *Tarzan*, "As Sun Turns To Moon," was written during rehearsals when one of the actors asked what his character was feeling at that moment in the story. As Phil began to think about it, he imagined it as a song and wrote it then and there.

DID YOU KNOW?

Every composer has a different way of working. Some write tunes first and then the lyricist fits in a lyric. Others write their own lyrics (like Phil Collins does), and still others sit in the same room as the lyricist so they can create the song together. Elton John likes to write the music to lyrics that have already been written. For *The Lion King*, Tim Rice faxed Elton the lyrics to the song "Circle of Life," and Elton wrote the melody in twenty minutes! The legendary duo is pictured here, working together at the piano.

Composer Alan Menken with The Little Mermaid lyricist Glenn Slater (above). Brothers Richard Sherman and Robert Sherman (below) wrote songs for Walt Disney as a team—both words and music.

This duo has been writing songs together for over twenty years!

ANTHONY DREWE AND GEORGE STILES

LYRICIST

The **lyricist**'s job is to write the words that go with the composer's music. Sometimes the composer is also the lyricist, but many of the most famous songwriting teams split the job between writing music and lyrics.

Lyricists share the job of revealing the plot and the characters' thoughts with the playwright. Sometimes the lyricist is the playwright, too.

Lyrics are like poems set to music. They are often very beautiful even when read without music at all. Some lyricists write the words to the song first and then give them to the composer. Other times the composer comes up with a musical idea and shares it with the lyricist, who comes up with a lyric to it. Some writing teams share the responsibility of both the lyricist and the composer, with each person dabbling in song and lyric writing. However they create the song, all that matters is whether it is any good.

Often, the lyricist has the job of turning spoken scenes into songs between two characters. Other times songs are written for just one person—as if they were sharing their inner thoughts directly with the audience.

Some lyrics change a great deal while the story of a show gets worked out. The tune can stay the same, but the lyricist, like the playwright, must keep writing and rewriting. Lyricists have to know a great deal about poetry, a great deal about playwriting and character development, a great deal about song structure—and a great deal about patience.

Ask any lyricist, and he'll tell you why that last bit matters.

Brilliant lyricist Howard Ashman died before his film Beauty and the Beast opened, but his words live on every night onstage around the world.

Stage Notes

★ For the stage musical of *Mary Poppins*, Anthony Drewe wrote original lyrics for brand-new songs like "Practically Perfect" and "Anything Can Happen If You Let It," as well as new lyrics for well-known songs like "Supercalifragilisticexpialidocious," "Jolly Holiday," and "Step In Time."

★ *The Lion King, Beauty and the Beast*, and *Aida* lyricist Sir Tim Rice often writes "dummy lyrics" to get the rhythm right for the composer. He then goes back and writes the real words later, after the music is finished. It can be a big laugh when you hear the very silly words he's written as dummy lyrics for some very famous songs.

★ The *Beauty and the Beast* album was recorded while the show was still in previews, and contains slightly different versions of the songs that ended up appearing onstage, including an entire section of one song that has since been cut.

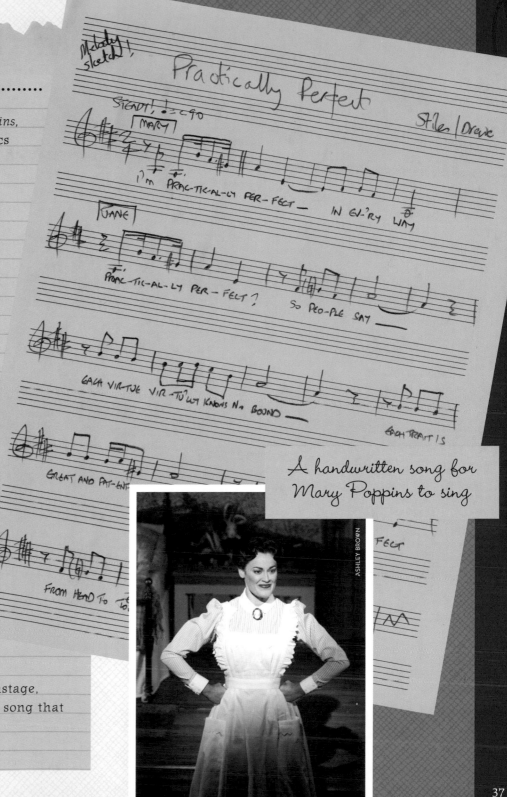

A handwritten song for Mary Poppins to sing

PRODUCER

The **producer** has one of the hardest jobs in the theater to describe or understand. Basically, the producer is the one who decides to put on a show and decides what the show is. He then assembles the people to do it (the playwright, director, designers, actors, and everyone else) and supervises their work. The producer is usually held responsible if the show fails but is often ignored if it is a success—except by his friends, of course.

You may think that the director and the producer both sound like the "boss" of the theater, but the difference is that the director is the boss of what happens onstage, whereas the producer is in charge of overseeing things that need to be done *beyond* the stage. It is the producer's job to arrange for everything that the production will require—from staff, to rehearsal space, to a theater. The producer also oversees the marketing, the advertising, the publicity, and the ticket sales.

Producers sometimes have very strong creative ideas about the production and work closely with the director, writers, and designers. Other producers are more businesslike and supervise the logistics, leaving the creation of the show to others. No matter what, the producer is held responsible for the show's success.

The reason why the producer literally "runs the show" is because he is also in charge of getting and managing the *money*. The producer sets the budget for the show and collects the money either from investors, companies, or even his own bank account.

However, there is much more to producing than writing a check, coming to a few meetings, and putting on a tuxedo for opening night. Producers care deeply about the success of the show, and do their best to make sure everything runs smoothly.

"All the inspiration I ever needed was a phone call from a producer."

Cole Porter (1891-1964)

Producers never do anything alone. Here are some of my favorite partners: Peter Schneider and I, with our Tony® Awards for The Lion King (top); me with Michele Steckler and Rick Elice; and legendary producer Sir Cameron Mackintosh and I (left).

Stage Notes

★ One night when previewing a show called *On the Record* in Cleveland, Ohio, we decided one of the costumes for the leading man just wasn't right. I suggested that a shirt I had in my hotel room would be perfect. I ran back to my room to get it, and right before entering the stage, the actor put it on. For the next week, that's the shirt the actor wore until the wardrobe department could buy some exact replicas for the rest of the run.

★ Legendary producer Cameron Mackintosh started working backstage as a stage manager for the original London production of *Oliver!* In those days, stage managers also went on in the show for actors who were too sick to perform. Phil Collins (who wrote the music for *Tarzan*, remember?) was in the show at that time, and Cameron was Phil's understudy. Nobody could have possibly known then all the great things that were to come for both of them!

This is MY shirt, but it looks a lot better on Andrew Samonsky (pictured here with Meredith Inglesby & Keewa Nurullah)!

★ I went to school to pursue a career in theater. I planned to be both an actor and a director. During the final bow of the last musical I appeared in, *Pippin*, I suddenly realized that I never wanted to act again and wanted to be a producer instead. I walked off the stage, took off my wig, costume, and makeup, and never performed again. I went back to school and dedicated myself to one day having my own theater company to run, which is what I do at Disney today.

★ Many producers are too nervous to sit down with the audience and watch a show. Cameron Mackintosh has never sat through an entire performance of *Mary Poppins* on Broadway without spending at least part of the show pacing in the back of the theater. (Neither have I, for that matter.)

Jim Abbott (above) has conducted both Tarzan® and Aida. (Below) Paul Bogaev knows how to get the band's attention with just his eyes!

MUSICAL SUPERVISOR & CONDUCTOR

There are a few jobs in the theater that have a number of titles. The music department is where a number of the jobs overlap. Some shows have such enormous amounts of music that there are many areas of the music to oversee. Brand-new musicals that have never been performed before are particularly complicated, because the songs, the underscore (the background music), the overture (the music before the curtains go up), and the dance music all need to be sorted. The music played by different instruments needs to be assigned and written out, the orchestra needs to be taught the new music, and the singers need to learn what they will sing. For big shows with all these musical elements, a **musical supervisor** coordinates everything.

Often, the musical supervisor is also the **conductor**, but not always. The conductor is a person everyone recognizes. He usually stands with his back to the audience, facing the orchestra and the stage. In most theaters, the orchestra is positioned between the audience and the stage, often in a slightly lower "pit" to avoid blocking the audience's view. The conductor's job is to set the pace or tempo of the songs and keep the orchestra and the singers all performing together. From his vantage point, he can see what's going on onstage and "cue" the musicians when to start. Very often the orchestra can't hear the singers at all, and sometimes the singers can barely hear the orchestra, so by watching the conductor, they can tell where they're supposed to be.

HOW THEY WORK

Try to imagine you are singing a song with a friend but you can't hear each other and you can't see each other—maybe your friend is in the next room. How do you know when to start, or if you're singing faster or slower than the other person? The conductor is the one who keeps the music all together and sounding great. Conductors also have to have very strong arms because they wave them around all night! It can be a very strenuous workout to conduct a show—almost like taking an aerobics class at the gym.

Sometimes all the orchestra members can't fit into the orchestra pit. Other times the sound can't be properly controlled, with loud instruments playing next to quiet ones. For *Aida* on Broadway, two violins, one viola, one cello, and a keyboard were all located on the seventh floor of the theater in a small room. The conductor watched them on a video monitor and the musicians watched him conduct on their own monitors. Each of the musicians played into a microphone and all of the sound went through the sound department's console to be "mixed" together. No one in the audience ever knew that some of the musicians were seven floors away.

With the front row so close, many conductors and orchestra members can carry on conversations with people in the audience before the show and at intermission. Once, conductor Paul Bogaev was hit on the head with a program at the end of a show by an elderly lady who was unhappy that the leading man died in the final scene. Apparently she didn't realize that he didn't write it, he just conducted it!

Stage Notes

* Paul Bogaev was an accomplished pianist and actor when he came to New York. He was pursuing a career in acting, and to make extra money he began taking jobs as an "audition pianist" who plays for singers when they audition. Eventually he was offered a job conducting at Radio City Music Hall and became one of the most respected music supervisors in stage and film.

* One night during the performance of a Broadway show, Paul had to catch a flying champagne bottle that was bouncing off the stage and heading right toward the head of a violinist. Conductors get good at catching all sorts of props that are heading into the orchestra pit. If you look closely, there are often big nets (sort of like fishing nets) over the orchestra to stop stuff (and people) from falling in.

David Caddick supervised the music on many legendary shows, including Mary Poppins.

41

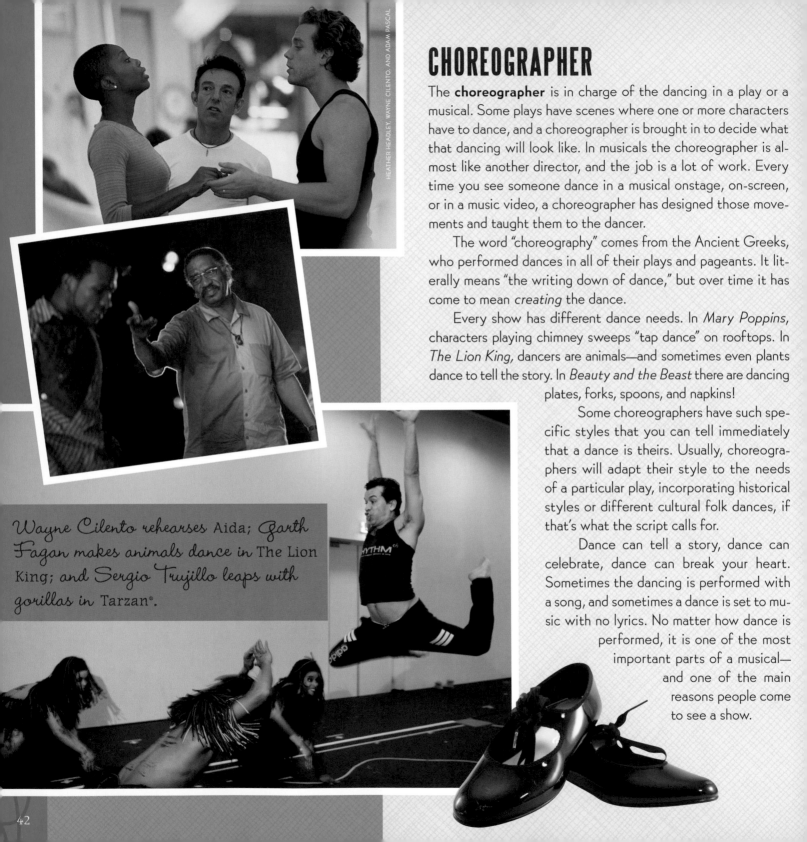

CHOREOGRAPHER

The **choreographer** is in charge of the dancing in a play or a musical. Some plays have scenes where one or more characters have to dance, and a choreographer is brought in to decide what that dancing will look like. In musicals the choreographer is almost like another director, and the job is a lot of work. Every time you see someone dance in a musical onstage, on-screen, or in a music video, a choreographer has designed those movements and taught them to the dancer.

The word "choreography" comes from the Ancient Greeks, who performed dances in all of their plays and pageants. It literally means "the writing down of dance," but over time it has come to mean *creating* the dance.

Every show has different dance needs. In *Mary Poppins*, characters playing chimney sweeps "tap dance" on rooftops. In *The Lion King*, dancers are animals—and sometimes even plants dance to tell the story. In *Beauty and the Beast* there are dancing plates, forks, spoons, and napkins!

Some choreographers have such specific styles that you can tell immediately that a dance is theirs. Usually, choreographers will adapt their style to the needs of a particular play, incorporating historical styles or different cultural folk dances, if that's what the script calls for.

Dance can tell a story, dance can celebrate, dance can break your heart. Sometimes the dancing is performed with a song, and sometimes a dance is set to music with no lyrics. No matter how dance is performed, it is one of the most important parts of a musical— and one of the main reasons people come to see a show.

Wayne Cilento rehearses Aida; *Garth Fagan makes animals dance in* The Lion King; *and Sergio Trujillo leaps with gorillas in* Tarzan®.

Stage Notes

* There used to be separate dancing and singing ensembles in a Broadway chorus. Today, all chorus members are expected to be both skilled singers *and* dancers.

* Each week, *The Lion King* cast uses nearly 100 ice packs to help dancers injured during the performance. The show may look pretty from out front, but sometimes it feels more like a hockey game backstage.

* The Broadway casts of both *The Lion King* and *Tarzan* have full-time physical therapists as part of their staffs.

* The more diverse skills a dancer has, the more likely he is to get work. Ballet, tap, modern, jazz, and gymnastic tumbling are all dancing skills that are used nightly in different Broadway shows.

* Garth Fagan was born in Jamaica, and is best known as a modern dance choreographer with his own company of dancers. *The Lion King* was the first Broadway musical he ever worked on, and he won the Tony Award.

* Stephen Mear, who was one of the choreographers on *Mary Poppins,* has a very close friend who is deaf. The idea of the choreography for the song "Supercalifragilisticexpialidocious" came from his experience with sign language. Onstage, the actors "spell out" the word in a sort of sign-language style.

Australian Meryl Tankard with her associate Leonora Stapleton (above); lionesses learn to "hunt"; and Stephen Mear (below with Kevin Samual Yee) kept the cast of Mary Poppins tapping on the rooftops!

STAGE COMBAT AND WEAPONS

Frequently onstage, actors have to create the illusion that a fight is taking place. That fight might be between two kids in school, two guys in a bar, or twenty guys in the 1500s. They may just swing fists, they may swing swords, or they may have to shoot guns. No matter what sort of fight it is or what sort of weapon they are using, the fight director is responsible for it. Sometimes, a fight can be something as simple as a leading lady slapping her leading man. But if she gets her move wrong, the leading man won't be leading anything but a bloody nose for the rest of the night.

Fight directors stage every swing, every step, every jump, and every blank bullet that comes out of a gun. Everyone who works in the theater knows that stage fighting and weapons are special skills that require meticulous attention. It has to look dangerous to the audience, but the actors need to feel completely safe at all times.

The fight director is also telling a story. Rick Sordelet, a professional stunt coordinator, says stage violence happens when characters can no longer articulate their conflict verbally, instead resorting to physical action. For example, in *Aida*, to save her friends from capture, the title character grabs a soldier's sword and holds it to his throat, demanding that her friends be released. The villain in *Beauty and the Beast*, Gaston, grabs a knife and lunges for the Beast to kill him in the final battle. Evil Uncle Scar lunges at Simba in *The Lion King* in a failed attempt to take over the pride. And in *Tarzan* the villain Clayton pulls a rifle on Tarzan to take him back to England as his prisoner, and Tarzan rips the rifle from his hands while tumbling across the stage. These are all scenes Rick has *staged*, and it's important that they happen exactly the same way every night (just like dancing) so that no one gets hurt. Rick teaches the essential theater lesson that the actors need to create characters that are *living truthfully under imaginary circumstances*. The fight may be completely imaginary, but it must be completely truthful for the audience to accept it.

Tarzan's carefully rehearsed moves look like a real fight onstage!

44

Stage Notes

★ When it needs to look like someone is being cut with a knife, actors often use a plastic knife with a tube running inside it. The handle gets filled with fake blood, and when the actor squeezes it, the "blood" oozes out wherever he puts the knife.

★ Every night before *Tarzan* there is a "fight call" where the actors who will participate in the fight that night have to go onstage and run through each of the moves just to make sure everything is safe.

★ Rick Sordelet not only stages the fight, but he also has to stage the resting during the fighting. For one show, the fight between two characters was so long that he had to build moments into the choreography for the actors to catch their breath. Otherwise they would not be able to continue with their lines when the fight was over. The challenge was to do that without making it look like the characters were resting.

Rick demonstrates moves for a fight scene in *Tarzan*®.

★ For one production of *Romeo and Juliet*, Rick had an actor wear a large packet of blood near where his front pocket would be on his pants. There was a pump attached to it and a long, thin, tube running from the packet to a spot on his back, so that when he was stabbed in the back at the end of a long sword fight it would look like the blood was "spurting." In the first performance, the actor lunged a bit lower than normal before anyone had even touched him and the bag of fake blood burst open, flooding the front of his pants. You can imagine what that looked like—and it certainly didn't look like he was stabbed in the back!

PUBLICIST

Every show needs publicity. Usually lots of it. Publicity is free "hype" about a show—it's everything people see and read about a show that the producers don't have to pay for. For example, producers pay to have advertisements in the paper, but if the paper writes an article about the show, it's free publicity.

The more publicity you can get, the less advertising you have to pay for. That's why a good publicist can be very valuable. The **publicist** is in charge of creating publicity opportunities for the show. The publicist also arranges for critics to come view the show, which creates more publicity when they write their reviews.

Sometimes the publicist organizes an event—maybe arranging for the cast to make a special appearance at a store or give a concert in the park—to get the public's attention and hopefully even get a reporter to write an article about it.

Sometimes publicists put on what's known as a "publicity stunt," where they arrange for something crazy about the show to look like it "accidentally" happened. When *Mary Poppins* was rehearsing for its pre-London tryout, the publicist knew that a nearby academy that trains nannies was having its annual graduation. The publicist sent the actress who was playing Mary to attend the event, and it suddenly made national news and brought attention to the show, which was about to open.

Next time you read an article about an upcoming show, see if you can figure out whether it happened by chance, or if it was just a stunt arranged by a publicist.

Of course, it is usually best to get *good* publicity, where people say nice things about the show to build interest and encourage the public to buy tickets. However, if you can't get good publicity, terrible publicity may save the day by making everyone wonder how the heck things can be so bad! Bad publicity is never a producer's first choice.

Most publicity comes easily when a play is opening, but for plays that run a very long time (often many years on Broadway) it is harder and harder to get attention for a show, and publicists can get very desperate. Nobody said it was an easy job!

A publicist can't make people say nice things—but the publicist is always blamed for it if they don't!

"There is only one thing in the world worse than being talked about, and that is not being talked about."

Oscar Wilde (1854-1900), from The Picture of Dorian Gray

Press photographers love opening nights; Rick Miramontez keeps actress Lynn Redgrave focused; and these sails were a great stunt to get attention for The Lion King in Australia.

Stage Notes

★ When veteran publicist Chris Boneau was in college and acting in a production of *Oedipus*, he looked out into the audience and realized that there were not enough people in the theater. He started to think about ways to attract more people to the show. He realized he must be a terrible actor because he was thinking about publicity when he should have been thinking about acting. He walked off the stage and went into the publicity business.

★ When former teen star and pop legend Donny Osmond performed as Gaston in *Beauty and the Beast*, publicist Rick Miramontez placed dozens of interviews and articles in New York–area publications. These articles were simply about Donny joining the cast of a show that had been running more than twelve years. If Donny had not joined the cast, none of those articles would have been written. Was it a good idea to cast Donny and get the extra press? You bet!

Chris Boneau knows a good publicist needs to keep smiling.

★ When Ashley Brown was cast to play Mary in *Mary Poppins*, she was already starring in *Beauty and the Beast* in the lead role, Belle. I called the publicist and advised him of the news, but told him to hold the story. I then went to Ashley's dressing room before her performance as Belle to tell her the good news. Although I knew Ashley could keep the secret until the official announcement was made, I also knew that everyone in the theater saw me come in, close her door, and then leave after much joyful screaming from the leading lady. By the time I got to a nearby restaurant for dinner, word had already spread all over Broadway that Ashley was the new Mary. The press began to pick up the story, and it got much more attention than if a standard press release had been sent out.

★ Once when legendary actress Eartha Kitt (voice of Yzma in *The Emperor's New Groove*) failed to show up at a radio interview for her big Broadway show, her publicist did an impersonation of her voice and did the entire interview without her. That's one skill they can't teach—resourcefulness!

SET DESIGNER

The **set designer**'s job is to take the audience on a visual journey by creating the world of the play. Everything on the stage except the actors and what they are wearing is a creation of the set designer. Sometimes stage sets and scenery are very literal, meaning that they look *literally* like real life. You might think, "Gosh, that looks just like a living room in a real house!" Other times the scenery is there to evoke a feeling about a place—or to suggest no place at all. It might just be a pile of dirt or blue carpeting across the floor and up the walls. These are all choices the set designer makes.

The designer's challenge is that he can't move the audience around, so he has to think about how to position the scenery to give the audience the best view. When you see a movie, the camera—the "point of view"—is always moving, but with a play the point of view doesn't change because you have to stay in your seat! The designer must make sure that each person gets the most impact possible from that one view.

The set designer also needs to think about what style of theater his set will be on. He designs a very different set for a thrust stage than he does for an in-the-round or proscenium production.

Some plays are performed entirely with one set. Other plays have many sets that change during the performance. The designer not only has to figure out what is onstage, but also how it all fits backstage.

Sometimes scenery is designed to move behind the curtain, where you can't see how it is done. Other times it is moved by people or machines—or even sometimes by the actors right in front of you. These are all choices the designer and the director make to communicate what they want you to think and feel about the world they are creating.

The scenic designer and the lighting designer depend on each other a great deal. Without the lighting designer, no one would see the set. Lighting can also make the set look glorious or terrible. On the flip side, if there is no set, the lighting designer has very little to light.

Bob Crowley first draws his ideas on paper before his designs are turned into models of the set.

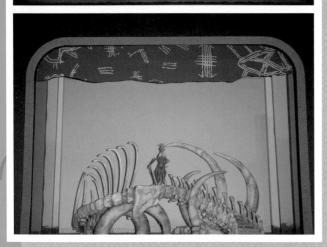

SET MODELS

Set models are like dollhouse versions of what will become the full set of a show. They are very valuable tools that help the designer show the producer, director, and choreographer what the show will look like, and how and where all the scenery will move. Set models help the director visualize where he will put the actors before the scenery is built, and they act as a guide for the people who will build the life-size set.

In rehearsal, actors only work with the barest elements of the set, and don't see the completed one until it is installed in the theater. Models are sometimes the only way everyone can tell what a set will look like before it is built—and after it's built you can't make changes!

Bob Crowley's Mary Poppins *model* (top), *and Stan Meyer's of* Beauty and the Beast (below)

Tarzan® and Aida set models by Bob Crowley, and one of Richard Hudson's models for The Lion King (top to bottom)

Stage Notes

* In Shakespeare's time, there were no sets at all. The actors would suggest in their lines where they were. "Oh, my, this storm is blowing so hard I think this ship might sink" could be a line to suggest where the play was taking place. You wouldn't have to build a boat onstage at all. (Then again, the actor would have to say something a lot more interesting than just that dumb line if there was no scenery to look at all night.)

* Bob Crowley says that the hardest part about designing a set is reading the script. Plays are written to be performed, and a script doesn't yet have the personality of the full production. It is really a skeleton of the production, so set designers really have to *imagine* the scenes while reading them.

* In *Mary Poppins*, there are two child actors named Jane and Michael Banks who have to enter their nursery thirty feet above the stage and ride in it while it's lowered to the floor during one of the scene changes.

* Many Broadway plays have complicated sets that require computers and motors to make all of the scene changes. One night during *Mary Poppins* in London, the scenery broke down, so the stage manager told the audience to wait while they fixed it. But the law in England requires child actors to leave the theater by 11:00 p.m. Due to the delay, two main characters, Jane and Michael Banks, were not even *in the theater* to play their final scene, so the actor playing their dad, Mr. Banks, improvised by stuffing pillows in their beds before the lights came up, and just pretended they were asleep.

* Everyone who works in the theater has stories about things that go wrong with scenery. When it is actually happening in front of the audience, it's terrible. But soon after, people can't wait to tell the story of how they cleverly survived the "disaster." Everyone tries to tell a story more wild than the one before it about these crazy nights.

> **"The scenery in the play was beautiful, but the actors got in front of it."**
>
> Alexander Woollcott (1887-1943), critic and commentator

SET DESIGN PROGRESSION

Look at this set designed by Richard Hudson from *The Lion King*, as it goes from sketches to its appearance onstage!

2. then comes the set model . . .

1. First the designer sketches the set concept . . .

3. then the set is built at the scene shop (that's director Julie Taymor testing it out) . . .

4. . . . and finally the set is used in a live show!

53

Sound designers, like John Shivers, need to know what every one of these buttons does!

SOUND DESIGNER

Theater has always had sound. When actors speak they make sound, a slamming door makes a sound, and an instrument makes a sound. In the theater, the person who makes sure you hear all of those things is the **sound designer**. Sometimes he just makes everything louder by playing it through a microphone, but sometimes he has to create the sound from scratch, like recording and playing back the sound of rain.

Once upon a time, everything you heard in a theater was created *live* by somebody. There were no microphones to make things louder or recorders to play back sound effects. Of course, once upon a time, there was no electricity for lights, or heat to keep the theater warm—or even a good place to take a shower, to make it easy to sit next to the stranger who bought the ticket for the seat next to yours!

Theater is more fun today, if you ask me.

Today, sound designers have the complicated job of managing or creating all of the sound you hear. In Broadway musicals, most actors wear tiny microphones to amplify their voices. The instruments in the orchestra are played through microphones, and the sound effects are all recorded. The sound designer figures out exactly what equipment to use and exactly where to place it so the sound is good in every seat in the theater. They also make sure that the sound is well-blended and balanced so that the audience hears everything just right.

Sound designers need to know a great deal about a lot of high-tech equipment. Their job is a lot harder than turning the stereo up or down. Sometimes there are more than sixty live microphones onstage and in the orchestra pit at one time! Each has to be balanced with the other, or you'll hear the third girl on the left instead of the leading lady during her big song—and trust me, the leading lady won't be happy about that!

They also need to have very sensitive hearing to be able to make everything sound natural and like it's coming from the stage. They also need to be storytellers who know exactly what sound to play and when. What type of gunshot should be heard? Is that the sound of a lion or a jackal in the distance? What sort of birds live in that part of the country and would be singing outside the window?

Stage Notes

★ Every night in *Tarzan* on Broadway, the sound of the baby Tarzan crying is actually Ruby, who is the daughter of sound designer John Shivers. He recorded it when she was seven months old. We didn't ask how he made her cry.

★ When everyone onstage is wearing tiny wireless microphones, it is essential that the mics only be on when that person is talking or singing. If they are all left on at other times, each microphone will pick up random sounds onstage. Worse, if they are left on when the actors are backstage, just imagine what the audience might overhear!

★ At the Old Vic Theater in Bristol, England, which was built in 1766, there is a long, curvy metal slide that runs above the ceiling, over the audience, and down to an offstage area. It is just the size to fit a cannonball. It was invented for the storm scene in Shakespeare's play *King Lear*, and when you put a cannonball into the slide and let it take its long and winding journey to the stage, the audience hears what sounds like a thunderstorm rumbling overhead.

SOUND OPERATOR

The sound designer plans all the sounds before the show happens, but the sound operator executes the sound designer's plan while the show is actually going on. The **sound operator** is often a different person than the sound designer, but in smaller productions the same person might do both jobs. The sound operator is in charge of the nightly running of the sound department from distributing and testing the microphones and speakers, to controlling the volume of the sound heard during the performance. This job gets more and more difficult as the technology advances.

Watching a sound operator on a big Broadway musical is like watching a recording engineer mix music in a big recording studio. The operator also has to run all of the pre-recorded sound effects. And that's not easy. It takes a lot of hand-eye coordination to do it just right. If you are really good at video games, you might be a good sound operator because both things take similar skills. For example, you might find yourself having to push a button at just the right time to make sure the audience hears the sound of a breaking plate just as an actor smashes a fake plate over someone's head!

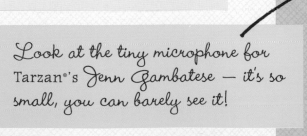

Look at the tiny microphone for Tarzan®'s Jenn Gambatese — it's so small, you can barely see it!

COSTUME DESIGN

A costume is everything the actor does (or does not) wear, and it is an important part of telling a story on stage.

The costume can range from a beautiful hand-beaded dress or shiny tuxedo to a complex body suit that makes an actor look like an ape. A costume can include masks and stilts, as with Julie Taymor's giraffe costumes in *The Lion King*, or it can feature giant, gilded cutlery, like Ann Hould-Ward's forks and spoons in *Beauty and the Beast*, or it can be as small as Bob Crowley's swimsuit-size loincloth design for *Tarzan*. How the costume looks and how it moves on stage are decisions made by the **costume designer** to help tell the story at hand.

Theatrical costumes tell the audience about the characters they are watching: whether they are young or old, a boy or girl, a doctor or a ditchdigger, rich or poor, shy or wild.

For instance, if you see a girl in a long white gown with a veil and a bouquet of flowers, you'd probably guess she's a bride at her wedding, but if you see her in that same costume but covered in mud, you can be sure something went wrong.

Costumes are often used to show the audience that the play takes place in a certain historical period or in a special location in the world—or out of it!

Costumes can even communicate the time of day or weather. If you see someone in shorts, sunglasses, flip-flops, and a T-shirt, you might think it's summer and they are at the beach. A long fur coat means it's winter.

Sometimes, a costume designer creates clothing that he or she thinks the character would actually wear if he was a real person. Every detail can be created to look absolutely realistic and natural. On the

DID YOU KNOW?

To play the octopus Ursula in *The Little Mermaid*, Sherie Rene Scott has two completely different sets of tentacles. We thought of them as her casual set and her "dress up" fancy set. Either way, they are very complicated to maneuver.

Stage Notes

★ Costumes are not just what you see onstage. Great designers also design the underwear and corsets for a character so that they will move and feel like someone who lived in that time period. Mean costume designers use itchy fabric.

★ The character of Mary Poppins arrives at the Banks family home and it is clear she really knows how to pack that small carpetbag. Not only does she pull a bed, a tall mirror, a large plant, and a hat stand out of it, but she also has to have room for her beautiful clothes, including a long purple coat, a long red coat, a long blue coat, and a number of blouses that she wears during the show.

★ A "quick change" is when an actor goes into the wings and has mere seconds to change her clothes before she comes back onstage. There are many tricks to the process, including wearing one costume under the other, Velcro fasteners that replace buttons, and lots of practice! And you better not be shy!! Jane in *Tarzan* has one change that she makes while running up five flights of circular stairs. She leaps out of her dress at the bottom, runs up the stairs in her Victorian styled "bloomers" and puts her new dress on just before she jumps into a hammock to be lowered thirty feet to the stage while she sings.

Designer Ann Hould-Ward's ball gown for Belle in Beauty and the Beast *weighs more than forty pounds.*

★ Over the past thirteen years, more than 70,000 quick changes have been perfomed in the wings at *Beauty and the Beast*.

★ A swing actor (see page 84) in *The Lion King* who covers both dancing and singing roles would need over twenty different costumes to be able to do his job.

other hand, theatrical costumes can be exaggerated or extravagant, creating a world of fantasy where the costume plays an important job in creating the visual wonder of a production.

Normally, the designer sketches the idea of what a character will look like, and a costume is built from scratch.

Sometimes the designer works with clothes from a large collection of costumes and "pulls" different items to mix and match into just the right look for a particular show. In the case of a production that is set in the present day, some costume designers will go to a variety of stores and "shop the show," buying just the right thing for each character. Before all those clothes got onstage, the costume designer had to make the choices of design, color, fit, and movement to create the character.

Costume designers are also responsible for making the clothes look "lived in" and the proper age. They will often add wrinkles and stains and sweat marks. They will sandpaper edges and tear at the fabric to make it look worn out.

Costume designers work very closely with makeup and hair and wig designers to create the complete look of a character.

The moth in Tarzan® wears a costume made with high-tech digital printing. The special technology allows a photograph to be printed onto a piece of fabric, which is then sewn into a costume (above).

Inside the sketchbook are Julie Taymor's drawings for The Lion King. →

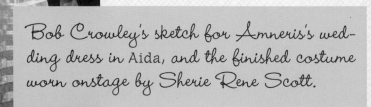

Bob Crowley's sketch for Amneris's wedding dress in Aida, and the finished costume worn onstage by Sherie Rene Scott.

AMNERIS – WEDDING   CROWLEY 1999

"I Just Can't Wait to be King"
SKETCHES & SWATCHES

JULIE TAYMOR • DESIGNER

HAIR & WIGS

You may know an aunt, uncle, teacher, or librarian who wears a wig. **Wigs** are head coverings made of real or artificial hair. Sometimes it's hard to tell they're fake; other times it's so obvious that it's fun. In theater, a wig is often part of an actor's costume. Wigs can conveniently hide baldness or change the color of an actor's hair. An actress with a short hairstyle can instantly have long, flowing locks, or an actor with a modern haircut can put on his hairpiece and step back in time.

The style of wigs and hairpieces can range from completely natural looking to larger-than-life and fantastic—depending on what's needed to tell the story and to communicate the character's identity.

Wig design involves two important skills: *making* the wig and *styling* it. A wig designer creates wigs for use onstage, and also designs moustaches, beards, and sideburns. Wig designers build each hairpiece to fit the actor's exact head measurements, and they style the wigs before every performance.

Like costume design, hair and wigs support the story, and help to visually identify the character, making his or her role more clear to an audience. A character's hairdo can say a lot about his or her personality and role.

Designer David Brian Brown fits Josh Strickland in his Tarzan "dreads" (above); Mary Poppins wig designer Angela Cobbin fits Kristin Carbone's wig (middle); actors all wear wig caps between their real hair and wigs (below).

KELLY REED, ANGELA COBBIN, AND KRISTIN CARBONE

Stage Notes

* Most Broadway wigs are made out of real human hair. The hair is bought all over the world—some people in small, faraway countries grow their hair just to sell it to wig makers. They may live on a farm in the Czech Republic, but their hair is starring on Broadway eight performances a week!

* It is impossible to make a wig with short hair. A wig designer always begins working with long hair, and then cuts it to the right length.

* In *Beauty and the Beast*, four characters have wigs designed by David Lawrence that are made out of yak hair: Mrs. Potts, Lumiere, Madame de la Grande Bouche, and the Sugar Bowl.

* The strangest wig David Brian Brown ever made was for a bunch of Broadway chorus girls who needed to have hairy armpits. He made little tiny wigs for them to put under their arms.

* The actress who plays Mary Poppins has rats in her hair every night! Not rodents, but little balls of wool or hair that wig designer Angela Cobbin has put into the wig to pad it out and make it fuller. You can't see them, but if she didn't have "rats" in there, her famous hat would crush the wig by the end of the performance and she wouldn't look like Mary Poppins anymore.

These wigs by David Brian Brown for The Little Mermaid *are built on "frames" so the hair stays up.*

CATHRYN BASILE, ZAKIYA YOUNG MIZEN, MICHELLE LOOKADOO, CICILY DANIELS, CHELSEA MORGAN STOCK, BAHIYAH SAYYED GAINES

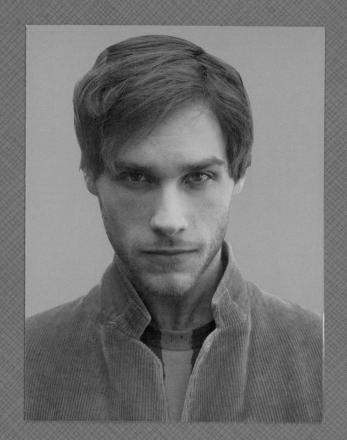

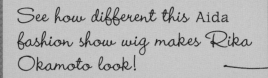

Look what a difference Tarzan's wig makes for Josh Strickland.

See how different this Aida fashion show wig makes Rika Okamoto look!

Hans Ligtvoet, who plays Professor Porter in the Dutch production of Tarzan®, wears a wig, mustache, and muttonchops (long sideburns)—all designed by David Brian Brown—that are held on with special glue. Notice how many different colors of hair it takes to make someone look like they have "gray" hair.

MAKEUP DESIGN

Everyone knows that actors wear makeup in the theater, but who decides what it looks like? All productions are different. For contemporary plays in modern dress, the actors and the costume designer or hair designer often sort it out for themselves and present the completed look to the director. But for a large, complicated show like *Beauty and the Beast*, *The Lion King*, *Tarzan*, or *Mary Poppins*, the job of creating just the right look for a boy raised by apes, a vain prince who has been turned into a beast, or a sooty chimney sweep falls on the **makeup designer**.

Most actors are trained to do their own makeup, but extreme makeup designs take a long time to put on and more than one person to help.

Some makeup, like a great ape named Kerchak in *Tarzan*, or the Beast in *Beauty and the Beast*, requires not only face paint, but also specially sculpted prosthetics—lightweight rubber pieces that get glued to an actor's face to change its shape and texture before the makeup is applied.

Makeup can tell more than one story at a time. The evil sea witch Ursula, in *The Little Mermaid*, sees herself as very beautiful, but at the same time she is frightening and bizarre. In this makeup design by Angelina Avallone (opposite page), Sherie Rene Scott shows both the glamorous and the scary side of the character. Notice how well the costume by Tatiana Naginova, the wig by David Brian Brown, and the makeup by Avallone integrate seamlessly to bring the character to life. It helps to have a brilliant actress inside it all.

Some makeup is worn on the body. This is, logically, called body makeup. Body makeup takes a long time to put on and is almost impossible to use in a show with a lot of costume changes.

In *The Lion King*, some actors change their face makeup more than a dozen times during the show, just like costumes. Some makeup designs, like that of the wise baboon,

DID YOU KNOW?

Makeup training takes many years. Naomi Donne (here with Ashley Brown), who has designed three major musicals for Disney, studied and then apprenticed for several years to learn her craft. She is trained in all forms of makeup, from making actresses beautiful to turning them into fantasy monsters.

Rafiki, in *The Lion King,* who serves as a sort of narrator for the show, take almost an hour to apply for each performance. The actress's face is painted with elaborate patterns that are filled in almost like an oil painting.

MAKEUP CREW

The makeup department recreates the makeup designer's creations nightly. They also make sure all the actors who apply their own makeup are doing it correctly and have the supplies they need to get it done.

The makeup crew members are also the "makeup police," making sure that no one is putting on too much just to get extra attention, or too little to make cleaning up after the show easier.

The makeup crew helps actors in their dressing rooms, in the makeup room, or backstage in the dark between scenes. It is very common for makeup artists to hold small "bite-lites" in their mouths, pointed at an actor's face, while they quickly make adjustments or changes backstage.

The makeup crew requires specialized training, and most great makeup designers started working on a makeup crew.

Angelina Avallone, seen here with Sherie Rene Scott, trained as a makeup designer in Florence, Italy.

Stage Notes

* More than eighty prosthetic makeup pieces are used in *Beauty and the Beast* and the Beast has used more than 3,300 latex noses and sixty sets of feet and hands. Makeup designer John Dods is in charge of all those fake body parts!

* Makeup artist Jorge Vargas says that makeup is not always for the audience—some details can't even be seen in the first row. Actors might need to wear "the mask" of makeup to help them get into character or feel like someone else. For *Aida,* Jorge waited in the wings each night for one of the actresses to exit the stage, and he made a very small change to her makeup before she went back out for a very emotional scene. This little moment gave the actress a chance to focus on the change the character was experiencing.

* As stage lighting has improved over the past two decades, stage makeup has changed dramatically. The better the light, the less makeup the actor needs to wear to distinguish his or her features.

* Naomi Donne had to design a special kind of body paint for the apes in *Tarzan.* They swing on vines and roll on the floor a lot, so conventional body makeup would have smudged or rubbed off. To get the liquid makeup to stay on the actors and not on the scenery, she mixed it with a few drops of surgical adhesive (glue that doctors use). It then stayed where it belonged until the actors washed it off after the show—with a *lot* of scrubbing!

Jorge gets Alex Rutherford ready to play young Tarzan on Broadway.

It takes almost a full hour every night for actress Tshidi Manye to become The Lion King's narrator, Rafiki. Broadway's original Rafiki, Tsidii Le Loka, demonstrates how the makeup looks with the full costume. The makeup was designed by Michael Ward.

No food in the theater . . .

. . . no yackin' during the show

blah blah blah blah

. . . no photography please

. . . and leave your big hat at home!

On With the Show

Now that you've found your seat and met some of the people that work on what you'll see, it's time to get ready for the show!

THEATER ETIQUETTE

Etiquette is a fancy way of saying "the way you are supposed to behave." Some people think they don't need to behave at all anymore. But etiquette helps everyone get along, especially in crowded spaces. People who are regular theatergoers know how to behave in the theater. Others need to be reminded. Soon, you'll be reminding people how to behave, because when they don't behave they ruin the event for everyone.

These are the basic rules. Read through this list and see if you agree. What have we left out? What rude things do people do in the theater that bug you? Feel free to add to this list!

Rule #1: Don't talk. Just don't. No one wants to hear what you have to say until after the show is over. This isn't TV, and you aren't at home. (It is perfectly all right to "shush" talkers, just like a librarian would do.)

Rule #2: Don't take photographs. The noise and the flash are disturbing to the audience and dangerous to the performers. If you want pictures, buy a souvenir program in the lobby. The same goes for video. (The one time it is perfectly okay to take photos is when your mom or dad or grandma or aunt or someone else who loves you soooo much they just can't stand it, wants to take pictures of you in a school show. THAT'S IT, THOUGH!)

Rule #3: You aren't an animal in the zoo, and you aren't in a restaurant. *Don't* bring food. If you must have a little something, like candy, make sure that there are **no** noisy wrappers.

A few more: Sit still and don't kick the seat in front of you. And don't wear big hats. People behind you need to see, too.

Now what's on *your* list?

The Play's the Thing

There are many kinds of shows. There are dramas set in historic times with large casts, and there are one-person plays. There are comedies set in the present day, and comedies that were written many, many years ago. There are musical comedies with loads of dancing and funny characters, and there are musicals that aren't funny at all. Some of the most popular musicals of all time don't have a laugh in them (unless someone falls down or breaks a prop by accident). Sometimes a show isn't a play *or* a musical, but a collection of songs that, when sung in a particular order, make sense in some way or mean something. For example, a collection of patriotic songs all sung together might make you feel good about the country you live in, or a bunch of romantic songs might make you feel romantic, or a bunch of songs about food might make you feel hungry—get the picture? That's normally called a revue. It can be hard to always put everything into a particular category, and that's probably a good thing. Not all ideas for shows fit neatly into the definitions set by what has come before. People are like that, too.

The following are some of the basic types of shows, so you'll know what people are talking about when you hear them.

DRAMA

Drama can mean a lot of things. "Oh, please, cut the drama," means stop overacting in life and just get on with it. Drama is also the universal art form of theater. Normally when we say a play is a drama, we mean that it is serious in nature and probably doesn't have a lot of laughs.

Tituss Burgess as Sebastian in The Little Mermaid; *the cast of our musical revue* On The Record; *and a tender love scene with Adam Pascal and Heather Headley in* Aida (*top to bottom*).

Sierra Boggess plays Ariel on sea and land—AND sings while skating on Heelys!

COMEDY

Comedies are funny. They make you laugh—or hopefully, at least, smile. A really, really funny play is clearly a comedy. Some older plays are called comedies when the topic isn't too serious, but frankly they aren't all that funny and you shouldn't expect to get a stomachache from laughing all night. Sometimes plays that are just lighter in tone are called comedies, too.

MUSICAL

Musicals are plays that use music to tell the story, and generally (but not always) mix up the songs with spoken words. *Beauty and the Beast* is a musical. So is *The Lion King*. Some people make the distinction between musical *comedies* and other types of musicals; some musicals aren't funny at all. *The Phantom of the Opera* doesn't have a lot of laughs, but people love it. The key element of musicals is that they tell their story in song.

CLASSIC

A **classic** is a play that was first performed long ago and still feels relevant today. To call something a classic is to give it credit for enduring because of its timeless meaning. The plays of Shakespeare are called classics because, although they were written more than 500 years ago, we still find relevance and truth in their stories. The same is true about great older plays from many countries that have been translated into languages for audiences all over the world. A classic can be a drama or a comedy. Some theater companies dedicate themselves to only producing classic plays, and they do them in all styles, including performing classic plays in costumes that look just like the clothes we wear today.

REVIVAL

A **revival** is a play or musical that is being done after the first production has run and closed. A revival is generally done by different people than the ones who did it the first time, and most often runs many years later. A revival can look completely different than the original, or it can look sort of the same.

WATCHING THE PLAY

There are a few tricks to watching a play.

If it is a classic, try to read it, or something about it, before you go. Sometimes the words can be hard to understand. The more you know beforehand, the easier it will be.

Use all of your senses. Listen, look, absorb it with every part of you. Allow yourself to be transported.

Most importantly, go in with an open mind. There's an old expression that applies to everything artistic, "You don't know what you like, you like what you know." It means you don't have a clue what you will like until you *get to know* it. The mind is like an umbrella—it won't work unless it's open! Keep that in mind every time you go to the theater.

OVERTURE

Some musicals start with a medley of the music you are about to hear, called an **overture**. It signals to the audience that it is time to pay attention (and stop *talking*, for pity's sake!), and hear some of the tunes that will be played during the evening. Not all musicals have overtures, but some of the best music ever written for the theater is in overtures. (At the start of act two there is often a miniature version of an overture. It's called the **entr'acte**. That's French for "hurry up and sit down, act two is starting.")

When the house lights go down and the curtain (if there is one) opens, it is one of the most exciting moments in the theater. The show is starting—and **anything** is possible. Enjoy!

INTERMISSION

Plays and musicals are broken into segments called **acts**. Most, but not all, musicals are broken into two acts. Plays are often in two acts, and some older ones are in three acts. Between the acts is a time to get a drink or stretch your legs. That break is called the **intermission**. In England, it's called the "interval."

If you are seeing a play with just one act, the program usually indicates that the show is presented "without an intermission." That's why I make it a habit to always visit the bathroom before the show starts. No one will ever give you better advice in life than that!

CURTAIN TIME

"Curtain time" is the time when the show starts. "What time is curtain?" means "What time does it start?" "Keeping the curtain up" means keeping the show going—even when things are going wrong—and "final curtain" means the time the show is over.

The usher rings a chime to signal the end of intermission.

71

CENTER STAGE

ACT TWO
Back of House: From the Stage Apron to the Stage Door

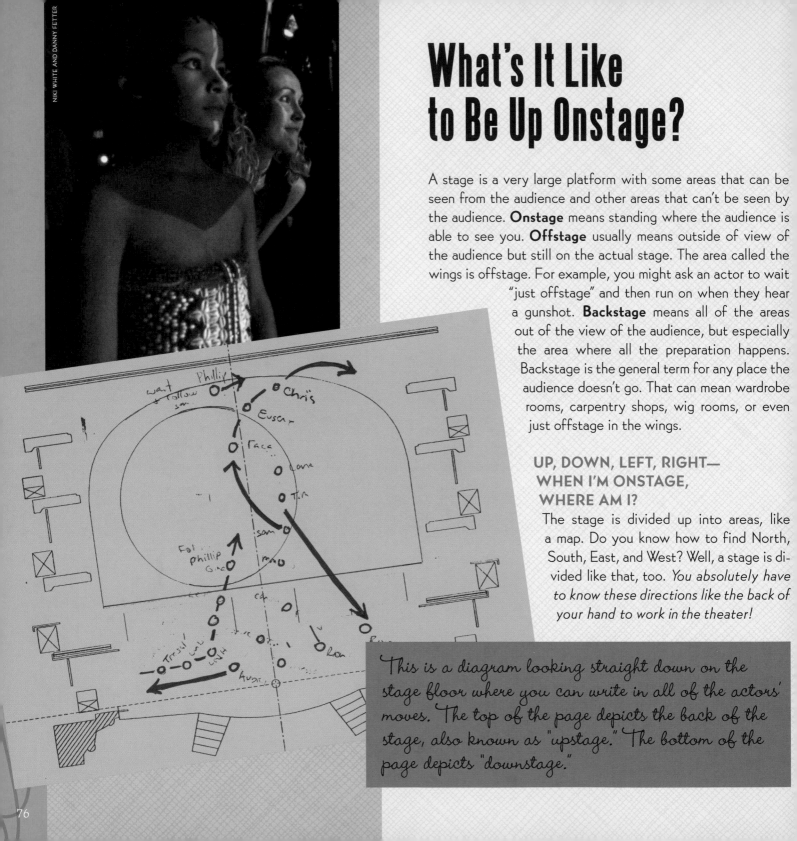

What's It Like to Be Up Onstage?

A stage is a very large platform with some areas that can be seen from the audience and other areas that can't be seen by the audience. **Onstage** means standing where the audience is able to see you. **Offstage** usually means outside of view of the audience but still on the actual stage. The area called the wings is offstage. For example, you might ask an actor to wait "just offstage" and then run on when they hear a gunshot. **Backstage** means all of the areas out of the view of the audience, but especially the area where all the preparation happens. Backstage is the general term for any place the audience doesn't go. That can mean wardrobe rooms, carpentry shops, wig rooms, or even just offstage in the wings.

UP, DOWN, LEFT, RIGHT— WHEN I'M ONSTAGE, WHERE AM I?

The stage is divided up into areas, like a map. Do you know how to find North, South, East, and West? Well, a stage is divided like that, too. *You absolutely have to know these directions like the back of your hand to work in the theater!*

This is a diagram looking straight down on the stage floor where you can write in all of the actors' moves. The top of the page depicts the back of the stage, also known as "upstage." The bottom of the page depicts "downstage."

- If you stand in the center of the stage you are standing **center stage**.

- If you are standing center stage and are facing the audience you are facing **downstage**.

- If you are standing center stage and facing downstage, the area behind you is **upstage**.

- If you are standing center stage, facing the audience with your back to upstage, you will find **stage right** on your own right and **stage left** on your left.

TO REVIEW:

Center is in the middle. **Downstage** is toward the audience. **Up-stage** is away from the audience. **Right** is to your right, and **left** is to your left *when you face the audience*.

DON'T THEY KNOW UP FROM DOWN?

Why is the upstage up and the downstage down? A long time ago (and even sometimes today), stages were sloped toward the audience, with the higher part away from the audience, and the lower part towards the audience. This helped the audience to see everything onstage. That slope is called a **rake**. When you hear, "Is the stage raked?" it means, "Does it slope?" Once you know that, and think about it for a minute (I'll wait), it is easy to understand why it is called **up**stage and **down**stage. The names of other parts of the stage are pretty obvious, aren't they?

TRAPPED!

There is one more location on the stage, and that goes straight down below the floor—through a **trap**. A trap is a hole in the floor that you can enter the stage from, exit through, or bring scenery or props through. There are many different kinds of trapdoors, and some stages have many of them; they can be very useful ways to create simple stage illusions or bring up entire rooms full of scenery. Some traps have "lifts" in them—they appear to magically "lift" the actor or scenery onto the stage, or make them disappear through the floor.

TEST YOURSELF!

Take a piece of paper and mark one of the long sides with a *D* at the edge. *The piece of paper is now your stage.* The *D* is the audience edge of the stage, or downstage. Now put a *U* on the opposite edge. That's upstage. You can now figure out where to put the *R* for right, *L* for left, *C* for center.

Mark where you think downstage right is. The director would say to an actor, "Now, I want you to walk downstage right when you say that line," and you know that that would be toward the audience, but also towards the right. Right?

Where is upstage left? Left of center? Where would you be going? The basic upstage, down-stage, stage right, and stage left positions can be used in lots of combinations. It's like a code.

NOW TRY THIS:

Find a place without a lot of stuff in the way, like an empty garage or a playground. Pretend it's a stage and decide where the wings are. Ask a friend (or more than one) to stand center stage, facing downstage. You stand where the audience would be, and start giving stage directions.

If you want your friend to go to your left, you need to tell them to go stage right because your left is their right when you face each other. The directions are always from the actor's side, and the director has to think backwards. Give lots of directions: upstage center, downstage left, have them enter upstage left and walk (or **cross** as we say in the theater) to downstage right. Switch roles, and let your friend be the director, and you be the actor. Can you keep your directions straight?

These casting directors know just about every actor on Broadway.

BERNIE TELSEY

TARA RUBIN AND ROBERT LONGBOTTOM

CHILDREN'S AUDITIONS!

Disney PRESENTS

THE LION KING

BROADWAY'S AWARD-WINNING BEST MUSICAL

STAR IN A SHOW!

Casting new performers for the Broadway and National Touring Companies.
Minimum weekly salary is $1,465*.

Seeking children ages 9–12, with a maximum height of 58", who can sing, dance and act to play the African lion cubs Simba and Nala. We encourage children of all backgrounds to attend. No performance experience necessary.

WHEN:
Saturday, November 4, 2006
Sign in: 10:30am
Sign in no later than 12:00pm

WHERE:
Screenland Studios
10501 Burbank Blvd.
(two blocks east of Cahuenga)
North Hollywood, CA 91601

Kajuna Shuford & Scott Irby-Ranniar, original Broadway cast, photo: Per Breiehagen

PREPARE:
Be prepared to be taught the last verse of Just Can't Wait to be King. All children must be accompanied by a parent or guardian. Parents or guardians must remain at the audition site at all times. Be ready to wait.

FOR AUDITION INFORMATION
Casting Hotline: (212) 627-5450 • www.lionkingcasting.com
If you are unable to attend this audition, send a picture and contact info ASAP to:
Binder Casting • Attn: The Lion King Kids • 321 W. 44th Street • Suite 606 • New York, NY 10036
www.bindercasting.com

©Disney

*Subject to applicable state laws regarding trust funds for minors.

How Can You Get Onstage— And Then What Happens?

CASTING

There are many elements in a show that need to be just right, or the show won't work. **Casting** is one of them. It isn't just about getting good actors. It's about getting an actor who's good for a particular role. Some of the best actors in the world are just not right for certain parts, and casting the right people is the job of the producer, the director of the play, and the **casting director**. The casting director is responsible for finding and bringing in potential actors for every role so that the producer and director can decide who can play what character.

Another tricky part of casting is that on a long-running show like *The Lion King* or *Beauty and the Beast*, you can't expect the original cast to stay with the show for years and years. That means that actors in all the parts—big or small—are always coming and going. Casting isn't just about who's onstage opening night. It's about who's onstage as long as the show is playing. So, what does the actor have to do to land a part?

AUDITION

Auditions are when actors perform in some way for the creative team of the show, to demonstrate that they are right for a certain part. All auditions are different, and because auditioning is so important (it's how you get the job, after all), there are whole books written about how to do it well.

For a musical, an audition usually requires singing, dancing, and acting. The director knows what she is looking for and structures an "audition process" that will help her find the best actors for that particular show. For example, when casting a show like *Tarzan* with a lot of apes onstage, she might ask actors to show that they can move around like a gorilla and walk on their knuckles or flip backward. Actors need to be ready for anything!

Most actors who work on musicals always carry a bag with them that has sheet music for several songs in different styles that represent how they sing. If the director wants a love ballad, the prepared actor has one ready to go. If the director wants a fast song with a rock beat, they have that, too. The same goes for shoes and clothes. Want to see me tap dance? I've got tap shoes. Want jazz or ballroom dancing? I've got shoes in here for that, too. If the show has a special requirement, like rollerskating, the actors are told that ahead of time so they can prepare.

Before auditioning for a play, actors are usually given a scene or two by the casting director—or whoever is in charge of the casting process—to prepare on their own and read in front of the director and producer. Sometimes during the audition, the director will suddenly ask an actor to read for the part of a character they were not called in to play or to read an unfamiliar scene. Again, the actor must be ready for anything.

Auditions test many things about actors. Of course they show how well an actor can perform, but they also reveal how well he can adapt to change or direction.

Auditions also teach the show's creators about their show. Sometimes it is the first time they will have seen any of the choreography or the first time they've heard someone other than the composer sing the songs. When Tony Award–winning actor Shuler Hensley auditioned for the role of Kerchak in *Tarzan*, he was a different type of actor than what the director was looking for. He didn't fit the character description that had been sent out, but the casting director Bernie Telsey knew he was a brilliant actor and singer. Shuler "reinvented" the character in front of the show's creators and was cast in the role. Because of his audition and interpretation of the character, new scenes and even a new song were added to the script, and the show will forever be better for it.

CALLBACKS

Once the actor is done auditioning, he must go home and wait for a **callback**. Callbacks are when actors audition a second (or third or fourth) time after the first audition. Usually many people audition, and as callbacks proceed, the selection gets smaller and smaller as you get closer to casting the show. At callbacks, actors may be asked to do the same thing again, or to play scenes with other actors who are also auditioning to see how they look together.

These are my notes from one day of casting on Tarzan®. If you don't write something about every person who comes in, you will forget who you liked.

telsey + company
311 West 43rd Street
10th floor
New York, NY 10036
Tel (212) 868-1260
Fax (212) 868-1261

TARZAN
The Duke @ New 42nd St. Studios
229 W42nd St.
Thursday, December 15, 2005

Accompanist: Chris Curtis
Reader: Ken Cerniglia

10:00   SHULER HENSLEY   Kerchak   Paradigm

Holy cow! such a different take on the character. Fantastic voice. Big say Bring him back!

MERLE DANDRIDGE – 1ST APPT   Kala   Harden-Curtis

REQ to sjust to see her grow. Even more Beautiful than during Aida. Great sensitive take on the song. Phil will love her.

10:10   JOSH STRICKLAND   Tarzan   Buchwald & Assoc.

Where did this guy come from? What a voice! w/ that hair looks like Tarzan. Can he move? Picture needs to fly him. He is sensational find.

10:20   JENN GAMBATESE   Jane   BRS

Love love love her. So much prettier than I remember from Elvis show & Hairspray. Great comic actress wonderful timing. Charming head to toe.

10:30   KEVIN MASSEY   Tarzan u-s   Buchwald & Assoc.

very interesting. Great voice. great look. another newcomer w/ a lot of talent. Bring him back.

Shuler Hensley gave a great audition for Kerchak in Tarzan®.

79

These chimney sweeps in Mary Poppins had to learn the dance and how not to whack each other in the head with their chimney brushes! Below, Cody Hanford learns his new song as Flounder in The Little Mermaid.

REHEARSAL

Once the cast is picked, it's time to get to work! The **rehearsal** process for every show is different, but no matter what the show is or who is in it, the rehearsals are the process of learning the script and learning what to do onstage. The director tries all of his ideas, and the actors try as many of their ideas as the director will let them. Rehearsals for musicals are a bit different from those for other plays because musicals need music and choreography. Most musicals rehearse in several rooms simultaneously—some actors practice the songs, while others work on scenes onstage, for example—to learn all of the different aspects of the production. Straight plays usually rehearse in one space. No matter how the rehearsals are done, by the end of the process the show should be ready to perform.

Rehearsals can be joyful or agonizing, and often are both. It is a time when everyone learns about each other and about the show. Behaving well in rehearsals when everything is constantly changing, lines and songs are being cut, and dances are being learned, undone, and relearned, is a very important part of working in the theater. If you don't like rehearsing, the theater probably isn't for you.

BLOCKING

Blocking is the process of telling the actor where to move and what to do. The director "blocks," or stages, the show, the actor learns the blocking by doing it and writing it in his script, and the stage manager records the blocking in her script so she knows exactly where everyone is and how they got there. Blocking is very important. Sometimes, actors forget where they are supposed to go. If you're lucky and the show is a hit, you'll have to teach the blocking to many other actors who will play that part.

LOAD-IN

While the actors are in the rehearsal room learning the show, the technical crew is **loading in** the scenery and lights. Load-in can be a simple process, like loading in a piano and a couple of stools, or it can take a couple of months for a large Broadway show, such as *The Lion King*. Compared to loading in permanent sets, as on Broadway, touring shows are designed (and rehearsed) to load in very quickly—sometimes even in eight hours. Ideally all of the scenery and lighting will be in place and operating perfectly before the actors arrive.

I've never seen that happen. Not once.

DRY TECH

Dry tech is a technical rehearsal where all of the scene changes and lighting cues are sorted out and practiced before the actors get on stage. It is a very useful process—in fact, it is an essential one.

It can be great fun during the dry tech to see a large piece of scenery move perfectly and gracefully on cue for the very first time. It is a lot less fun in dry tech to watch that massive piece of scenery crash into another large piece of scenery right before your very eyes. The only thing you can be happy about is that the actors weren't there to see it, too!

TECHNICAL REHEARSALS

These kinds of rehearsals can be long and slow and painstaking, as the entire cast and crew goes from the top of the show and rehearses every light cue, every scene change, every entrance, every moment of flying or stage magic, with all of the elements in place. This is where your nerves are tested. There is never enough time, everyone is anxious over whether or not the show

Rehearsals for Tarzan® took place in a very tall room where all the flying could happen. The floor is marked where the scenery will be placed throughout the show.

When looking out from the stage during tech rehearsals for Tarzan®, there is no audience, but the theater is full of "tech tables" so all the departments can work from the seats.

The best production supervisor in the business, Clifford Schwartz (right), deals with ten issues at one time.

is going to work, all usually seems lost, the hours are very long, nothing is working, and you wonder why you aren't working at a bank instead.

One of the most difficult technical rehearsals ever for a Broadway show had to be *The Lion King*. The show is massive, and there are so many costumes and puppets and masks to be organized and so much scenery to move around that it would drive anyone crazy. Very late one night, when the cast and crew had been rehearsing for many weeks and everyone was at their wits' end, Heather Headley, who was playing the girl lion, Nala, quietly began singing the song "Summertime" from the legendary musical *Porgy and Bess*. At first she sang just quietly to herself as she waited for a lighting cue to be sorted. People began to hear it, and all over the theater they stopped what they were doing and became quiet. No one said a word. Everyone just knew they were hearing something special from an actress who was destined for greatness. In that silent theater, her voice filled the space and reminded everyone why they loved the theater and why they were working so hard. When she finished, everyone erupted into applause and the technical rehearsals for that show changed just a little and became just a little easier.

By the end of **technical rehearsals**, the show should be able to go from first curtain up to final curtain in without stopping. I've never seen it go that well, but that's what is supposed to happen!

DRESS REHEARSAL

Dress rehearsals are when the actors perform the show in full costumes, wigs, and makeup, on the set with all the lighting, props, and scenery, just as they will be when the audience gets to see it. Often there are *many* dress rehearsals. The first one can be a total disaster as you try to put all the pieces together and learn what doesn't work.

Everything feels different at dress rehearsal: the wig causes an actress to get confused, the costume change is too slow between scenes, the actor didn't realize he wouldn't be able to put his arm around the actress because her dress is so gigantic he can't even reach her. . . .

You get the picture.

Performers

There are lots of categories of performers onstage, and there are different names for them. Whether male or female, singer, dancer, acrobat, or aerialist, everyone onstage is there to tell the story and make the audience believe, for just an hour or two, that there is a world on that stage that is worth paying attention to.

Everyone onstage is telling the story, and so to me, they are all actors. But here are the technical differences:

PRINCIPAL ACTOR

The **principal actors** play the main roles. They can also be called the leading actors. Some big roles are also referred to as "featured actor," meaning that it is a big part, but not *quite* as big as the leading actor. Some actors like to count the lines their character says in the show. Or count the songs. Some actors worry that the part isn't big enough. All they should really worry about is whether they are any good or not.

ENSEMBLE ACTOR

In a musical, an ensemble of actors plays many smaller roles and appears in the larger musical numbers. Once upon a time, the **ensemble** was referred to as the "chorus" and was separated into singers and dancers. Today, ensemble actors are expected to do both. Sometimes, a director will cast a brilliant dancer and ignore her singing, or cast an amazing singer and ignore his dancing, but they really have to be amazing in their specialty. Most ensemble actors need to be strong in both skills.

Also, many members of the ensemble cover, or understudy, the leading roles (more on that later). That second girl from the right in a production number just might be playing the lead role tomorrow night!

Recording star Toni Braxton played the principal role of Belle in Beauty and the Beast at one time.

The full cast of On the Record performed onstage with the band.

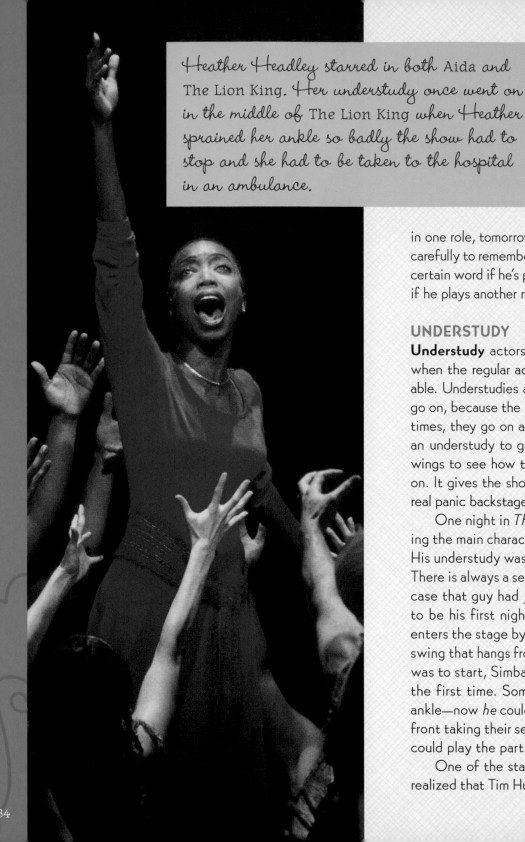

Heather Headley starred in both Aida and The Lion King. Her understudy once went on in the middle of The Lion King when Heather sprained her ankle so badly the show had to stop and she had to be taken to the hospital in an ambulance.

SWING

In musicals, one of the most exciting and challenging roles is the **swing**. Swing actors are called this because they can just "swing in" to any role during the dance and production numbers. The swings have many costumes, and they learn the choreography and songs from many different positions. Tonight a swing might be in one role, tomorrow another. He has to watch the show very carefully to remember that in the big number he turns right on a certain word if he's playing one part, but left on the same word if he plays another role.

UNDERSTUDY

Understudy actors (or cover actors) play the leading roles when the regular actor is either sick, on vacation, or unavailable. Understudies are often brilliant actors who never get to go on, because the person who they cover is never out. Other times, they go on all the time. Sometimes it's a big break for an understudy to go on, and everyone is watching from the wings to see how they will do. I love to see understudies go on. It gives the show a fresh energy—and sometimes creates real panic backstage.

One night in *The Lion King* on Broadway, the actor playing the main character, Simba, was sick and couldn't perform. His understudy was sick, too, and *he* couldn't perform either. There is always a second understudy on a big show, but in this case that guy had just started on the show. This was going to be his first night in the role. Well, the adult Simba first enters the stage by swinging from a rope—sort of like a rope swing that hangs from a tree. Thirty minutes before the show was to start, Simba raced onstage to rehearse this move for the first time. Something went wrong and he sprained his ankle—now *he* couldn't perform either. The audience was out front taking their seats and there was *no one* backstage who could play the part!

One of the stage managers did some quick thinking and realized that Tim Hunter, who had played a giraffe in the first cast of *The Lion King* and who had covered the role of Simba at that time, was now performing in another Disney show, *Aida*, a few blocks away. It was now almost time for the show to start. They called over to *Aida* and said they needed Tim, who was already in his costume and makeup, just about ready for the opening number. Simba doesn't enter until the end of act one so they rushed Tim to *The Lion King* theater, put his own understudy on for *Aida*, and got him out of his *Aida* makeup and costume and into his *Lion King* makeup and costume and onstage just in time for his first entrance. He had not played the role of Simba in almost two years and there he was in front of an audience that never knew anything had gone wrong!

Andy Pellick (above in the red shirt) is one of Broadway's top ensemble dancers. Jason Raize (right) was truly unforgettable as Simba in the original Broadway production of The Lion King.

A DAY IN THE LIFE OF A CHILD PERFORMER

by Henry Hodges

I am a kid living and working on Broadway. My regular routine is different from most kids but still regular. I go to school at the theater during rehearsals or I'm home-schooled. The kids I see every day are the ones I see at the theater, at auditions, and at dance classes. A lot of my best friends are actors, young ones and old ones. I spend a lot of time with adults, and I learn a huge amount from them. Most of my classes outside of school are filled with adults.

Most kids walk to school or take the bus. I ride my wave board to the theater. On the way I pass my neighbors, who work in the magic shop, candy shop, deli, and pet store in the neighborhood. I walk through the Hilton Hotel, where I know the doorman, Henri. I used to walk through the Edison Hotel, and I found my best tap teacher by talking with a cashier who works in the coffee shop there. A lot of actors stay at the Edison, and you get a discount with an Equity card. I used to get a candy discount in the lobby store.

Kids usually play team sports like basketball at school. I played for the *Beauty and the Beast* Broadway league softball team. I scored one run before a worried-looking woman ran up to me and said I had to be sixteen to be on the team. After that I was the batboy. But my run still counted.

At most schools, students take part in community service projects. Everyone on Broadway gives all year. My favorites are Gypsy of the Year, Easter Bonnet, Carols for a Cure, the Broadway flea market, and Broadway Barks. Just today I went to a talk-back at *Mary Poppins* for a group of kids with cancer.

From my apartment window on Fiftieth Street and Eighth Avenue, I can hear the bells at St. Malachy's Church play "There's No Business like Show Business" at half past every hour. To get to my library, I walk by Radio City and Rockefeller Center. Before I moved to New York to be in *Beauty and the Beast* I didn't even realize that there really were neon lights on Broadway, like the song says.

There are no holidays on Broadway unless they fall on a Monday. Sometimes people actually say "have a nice weekend" to you on Sunday night because Monday is our "weekend." I have done everything there is to do in New York on Mondays. My favorite is Monday Night Magic. It is a magic show, and every Monday it features a different mix of magicians.

In the summer, the show doesn't take a vacation like school. I love the beach, and I'm lucky there are so many beaches nearby. If you are not from New York, you probably don't know that you can get to Coney Island for $2 on the subway! It is funny to be in the middle of the city in your swimsuit, T-shirt, and a towel, get on the Q at 42nd Street, and 50 minutes later, you are at the beach. And I get to go on Mondays when it isn't crowded, even in the middle of August.

So, that is my regular routine. It has been an amazing adventure for me.

Henry as Michael Banks and Katherine Doherty as Jane Banks are hoping to find the "perfect nanny" in Mary Poppins.

Backstage

Only the performers and crew are allowed in the **backstage** area. So if someone from the show says to you, "Would you like to go backstage?" always say, "*YES!*" The show seen by the audience is no match for what happens "behind the scenes." All of the areas behind the curtains, on the stage, in the halls, or just places that are tented off from public view are referred to as backstage, even if these areas are not actually anywhere near the stage itself.

The mystery of backstage, of course, is that it's where the magic is created. It's where actors can be seen in costume but not "in character." "In character" means acting like the character and not themselves. In the performance you may see a sweet old lady who can barely stand, but backstage when no one is watching, that sweet old lady might be a beautiful young woman standing up straight and joking with her friends. The wig and costume and padding and cane may all be part of her costume, but backstage, before she is "in character," she isn't an old lady at all.

Stage managers, actors, crew and orchestra members, theater management, and other people who work on the show freely walk around backstage and see the show from a very different point of view. Sometimes the young lovers onstage can't stand the sight of each other when they are backstage, and other times the characters who fight like cats and dogs onstage might just be the best of friends when you see them backstage. You never know!

IF YOU HAD WINGS!

The sides of the stage, where actors stand hidden by curtains or scenery before they enter, are called the **wings**.

Wings are where some of the scenery is kept while it isn't onstage. Actors also stand in the wings before they enter or just after they have exited the stage. The wings can be dangerous because they are dark and scenery can come offstage *very* fast between scenes. If you are in the wrong place, you might just get run over by a castle, or a herd of wildebeests, or a bunch

You can look down the fly galley backstage and actually be above the flying actors in Tarzan®.

of chimney sweeps! Also, you have to be careful not to make noise that will distract the actors onstage or be heard by the audience out front.

The famous expression that someone is "waiting in the wings" literally means she is ready to go onstage. In real life, it can mean the person is waiting for her chance to be the center of attention. "She's waiting in the wings to become class president—just as soon as that obnoxious boy who's class president now moves out of town and gets out of our way!" Or something like that.

Tiny microphones are laid out backstage with each character's name on them.

Many front curtains are made of plush, red velvet.

"IT'S CURTAINS FOR YOU, MISTER!"

Cheesy gangster movies characters say that when they are about to kill somebody. It means, of course, that it's "the end" for someone. Well, the same is true in the theater—sort of. When the curtain goes up, it means things are starting, and when the curtain goes down, the show ends. But nobody gets killed!

There are as many different kinds of stage curtains as you can count on your fingers and toes—and your best friend's fingers and toes. There are curtains that separate the audience from the stage, there are curtains that block your view into the wings, there are curtains that are painted, there are curtains that are made of velvet, there are curtains that are designed so that you can see through them when the lights are adjusted in a certain way. Let's review the important ones. Of course, not all theaters have curtains—but when you need them, they come in handy.

MASKING CURTAINS

Masking is the most important job of curtains. Just like you wear a Halloween mask so no one can see your face, curtains in the theater cover things that we don't want the audience to see.

There are two main kinds of masking curtains, called **legs** and **borders**. Legs are the narrow curtains that "stand up" on the sides—a lot like your legs. Borders are the ones that hang sideways on the top. These special curtains hide lighting instruments and other things hanging above the stage, and also prevent you from seeing actors in the wings.

FRONT CURTAIN

The first curtain you are likely to see in a theater is the one that separates the audience from the stage. It hangs just upstage of the proscenium and has many names: show curtain, front cloth, main rag, act curtain, or house curtain.

There are two basic types of **front curtains**: The first kind go up and down, closing off the stage just like the blinds that raise and lower on your windows at home.

The other kind splits in the middle and opens side to side. These are like the fabric drapes that people sometimes hang over their windows instead of blinds.

BACKDROP

A **backdrop** is a piece of fabric that is stretched so tight that it looks like a solid wall. It hangs from a sideways pipe that can be raised or lowered. It is one of the most common forms of theatrical scenery. A backdrop can be painted to look like a forest or a city street or the inside of someone's house. Skilled painters can make them look three-dimensional and not flat at all.

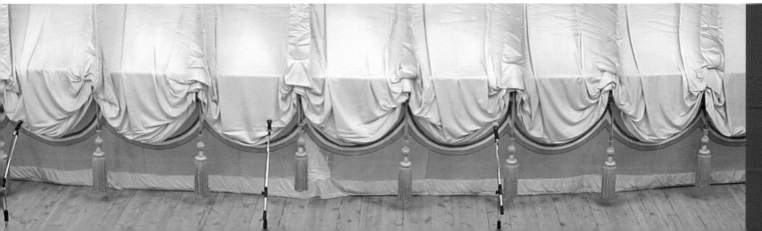

ANDREW SAMONSKY AND ASHLEY BROWN

ADAM PASCAL

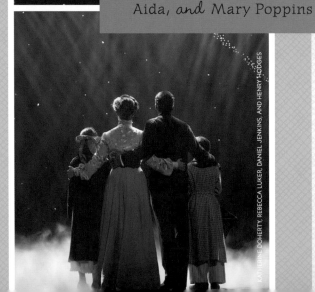

KATHERINE DOHERTY, REBECCA LUKER, DANIEL JENKINS, AND HENRY HODGES

STAR DROP

One of the simplest and most beautiful draperies onstage is the **star drop**. This is a large black or dark blue velvet curtain with tiny little lights (like white Christmas lights) pulled through it from the back. The wires are all hidden, so all you see are pin points of light in a field of darkness. It can look just like stars on a clear night.

You can see star drops in many shows. In *The Lion King*, the lion Mufasa makes a speech to his son Simba where he tells him to look at the stars. Onstage, Mufasa sings a song about the meaning of the stars, while the stars gently appear on a star drop hanging behind him.

SCRIM

A **scrim** is one of the most interesting curtains of all. It is made out of a special fabric; when lit from the front it looks like a normal painted backdrop, but when you light up what's behind it you can see right through it! Scrims can be one plain color or have a full scene painted on them. In *Mary Poppins*, we have a scrim that is painted to look like the outside of a house. When you light the scenery behind the scrim, the house disappears, and you look right through it.

SAFETY CURTAIN

The **safety curtain** doesn't have anything to do with the way the show looks. In fact, you hope the audience will never see it.

The safety curtain, sometimes called the fire curtain, is a fireproof curtain that closes off the stage area from the audience. Because theaters used to be very flammable, lawmakers decided that all the theaters should be required to have a fireproof curtain. If a fire were to break out onstage, this curtain would come down very quickly to keep the fire from going into the auditorium.

Fire has always been a big danger onstage. At one time, stage lights were gas-fueled flames, sort of like the lanterns you may use when you go camping. The scenery is frequently made of wood and other flammable materials. When you add to that the need for torches in some plays or candles in some scenes, everyone in the theater knows to be very careful with fire and fire safety.

CYCLORAMA

The **cyclorama**, or "cyc," is usually the furthest upstage curtain. Normally it covers the entire back wall, and unlike other draperies or backdrops it's usually completely blank. It is light-colored fabric and can be lit to look like the sky or just a beautiful color. The cyclorama sometimes is used to make the theater look like it's much deeper than it really is, because with just colored light on a vast expanse of fabric you don't have any specific image to focus on to tell how far away it is.

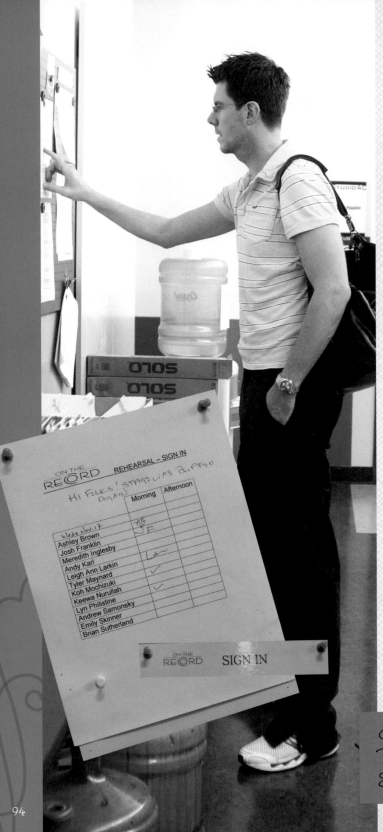

THE ROOMS BACKSTAGE

There are many different areas backstage where the actors and crew prepare for the performance. Every theater is different and many of them are cramped and old—not to mention drafty and badly heated, or full of bugs and rodents. Sounds glamorous, *no*? These are some of the spaces you'll find:

THE GREENROOM

The **greenroom** is where everyone gathers before going onstage. It's like a lounge or hangout. Very few Broadway theaters have greenrooms anymore. Space backstage in these old buildings is precious, and more important things always seem to occupy that space. But greenrooms often exist in *new* theaters.

The origin of the term "greenroom" is unknown, and theater people all make up crazy stories to explain it when asked. But the best answer would be "I have no idea," because *no one does!*

The most widely accepted origin of the term dates back to Shakespearean theater. Actors would prepare for their performances in a room filled with plants and shrubs. It was believed that the moisture in the plants was beneficial to the actors' voices.

DRESSING ROOMS

Dressing rooms are designed for just that—dressing. Actors either have their own room, or share them with others. Generally, the wardrobe department delivers a costume to the dressing room each night, and actors prepare for the show there by warming up and putting on their makeup, wigs, and costumes. "Star" dressing rooms range from glamorous to little hole-in-the-wall spaces. Sometimes chorus members all share one big room. Great actors know how to make the best of these small spaces. Many years ago a well-known actor named Yul Brynner had become famous playing the king in the musical *The King and I* on Broadway. He demanded his dressing room be painted a specific color of brown. He later toured America in this role,

Gavin Lee, who plays chimney sweep Bert in Mary Poppins, checks the call board. Everyone has to sign in on the call sheet (left).

and every theater he went to had to paint the star's dressing room "Brynner brown." Some of those dressing rooms stayed that color for many, many years, and other actors from then on knew they shared a dressing room with Yul Brynner!

STAGE DOOR

The **stage door** is where the cast, the crew, and anyone who works backstage enters the theater. They never come through the front door with the public. Traditionally, you will find three very important elements at the stage door.

The first is the **stage doorman**. On Broadway there is a long tradition of stage doormen who sit at tiny desks in tiny offices right next to the stage door. They monitor who comes in and out and keep track of deliveries. They keep out people who shouldn't be there and help people who *should* be there get where they're going. The stage doorman knows *everything*. He usually hears it all—intentional or not. Stage doormen can be the sweetest people in the world, and they always get a lot of respect from the cast.

Also at the stage door you'll find the **call board**, which is a backstage bulletin board that contains information about the production, including schedules for rehearsals and special notices. Everyone knows that it's their responsibility to check the call board *every day*. If it's posted there, you are responsible for knowing it. Theaters are too big to chase people down to tell them something. If there's news from the stage manager, actors find out at the call board.

Finally, at the stage door actors initial the **sign-in sheet**. Professional actors are required to be in the theater thirty minutes before the show starts. Some come earlier, but the rule is they must be there by "half hour." At thirty minutes to curtain, the stage manager checks the sign-in sheet to make sure everyone is in the theater. If someone has not signed in, preparations need to be made to put an understudy on. Lateness is never tolerated in the theater. Too many people are depending on you. *Including the audience!*

Stage doors are busy with actors arriving (top) and autographs being signed after the show (below); Jimmy Russell, the doorman, keeps things under control at Tarzan® (center).

WARDROBE ROOM

The people who maintain and prepare the costumes for each performance work for the **wardrobe department**. These people work very hard to clean, maintain, and repair (if needed), the costumes before each performance, and place them where they need to be. Some costumes are very elaborate and need daily attention. Buttons need to be sewn on, beads and sequins reattached, and zippers mended. All of this happens in and around the wardrobe room.

I have never been in a wardrobe room that didn't have a washing machine going. There is *always* laundry to do, and between costumes, undergarments, and the towels used to clean up after every show, the washing machine never gets any rest.

The wardrobe department is also responsible for getting the actors dressed. It is absolutely true that at home you are expected to get yourself dressed, and rightly so. But you don't have to get into a corset, or a flying harness, or a huge costume that lights up—that's what the wardrobe department is there to help with.

Very often, the wardrobe department doesn't deliver the costumes to the dressing rooms. Often they get "pre-set" around the stage for "quick changes" during the show. Frequently, actors race offstage and have to change their clothes in a matter of seconds. Shirts that open from the back with neckties attached to the front are torn off. An elaborate dress drops to the floor, and the actress steps right out of it and into another one. It gets lifted up and zipped with only seconds to spare before she races back onstage looking as if she were calmly entering on another day in the story. The wardrobe department conducts it all, and becomes very close to the actors.

Wardrobe people know when a sip of water is part of the costume change, or that on that particular night a cough drop is just the thing to keep the curtain up. Wardrobe people wear a sort of sewing version of a construction tool belt and are ready for anything from a torn costume to an actress who isn't feeling well and just needs to throw up before she goes back onstage. And yes, that happens—more often than you'd think!

Costumes have to be cleaned, repaired, and hung out in the wardrobe room (middle).

WIG ROOM

The hair department manages the **wig room**. It is no surprise that the wig room is where all the hair—wigs, mustaches, beards, sideburns, and occasionally hairy dog puppets—get maintained.

For a big show like *Beauty and the Beast* or *Mary Poppins*, there are literally hundreds of wigs in the wig room. Everyone needs their own custom-made wig, and frequently wigs get changed several times during the course of the show if the actor plays many different parts. Also, for each part played onstage, there are *three* people ready to play it, so that no matter who gets sick or goes on vacation, the show always goes on. And everybody gets his or her own wig! Lining the walls of the wig room are shelves full of wigs, all sitting on wig heads—which are like human-size doll heads with no faces.

Wigs can be very simple or very elaborate, and the hair department keeps them looking great. Every night at *Tarzan*, for example, the female lead Jane's wig gets reset, so that it looks just as fresh the next day. It's like a very fast-paced beauty parlor in there.

Wigs also get worn out, and new actors are always coming into the show, so just keeping track of what wig is on what person, which wigs are in the dryer, and which wigs need to be combed out is a big job. Now say "which wigs" ten times fast.

The hair department could easily get "wigged out" if they weren't organized.

Gary Martori has looked after all the wigs for On the Record, Tarzan®, *and* Mary Poppins; *he stores them on "wig heads" so they don't lose their shape.*

This tall wig for Mrs. Corry in Mary Poppins is made out of yak hair!

97

Special harnesses under actors' costumes allow them to "fly" suspended from wires.

THE LORD OF THE FLIES

In big theaters, "flying" objects—lights, scenery, curtains, o
props—are some of the most important tools of staging
play. Above the stage and out of sight of the audience is
fly tower, or **fly loft**. This is a huge open area often as big
and tall as the stage itself. It's like a box on top of a box. I
there's a twenty-foot-tall wall used as scenery on the stage
that scenery can "fly" twenty feet up inside the fly tower and
not be seen by the audience until it is lowered back to the
stage again. So, the fly loft is kind of like an attic where you
store things away while they're not being used.

There are two basic ways to make such magic—one is
with machines, and one is by hand. To fly things out onto the
stage by hand, ropes or cables are attached to the scenery

AHOY, MATEY! IT'S CURTAIN TIME!

Hundreds of years ago, stage designers wanted
to have elaborate scene changes, but they
didn't have any of the technology we have
today to make them happen. Flying scenery in
and out of view of the audience was a clever,
but complicated, idea. That's why sailors were
hired to develop ways to use flies safely, just
like raising and lowering the sails of a boat.
In fact, a number of things in the theater are
based on ships. The ropes and cables we use
are called "rigging," just like on a boat. Did you
know the stage floor is called a "deck," just like
the floor of a boat?

For this reason, it is also considered bad luck
for an actor to whistle on- or offstage. Sailors
used to use whistles on board ships to communicate with each other. Hundreds of years ago, an
actor whistling backstage might have mistakenly
cued one of the sailors to drop a sandbag that
could land right on someone's head!

lighting, or even a person. Those ropes go through a pulley and eventually end up tied off near the wall offstage. If you pull the rope, the object goes into the air. If you let go, it comes crashing down. That sounds like a disaster waiting to happen, doesn't it?

Well it *would* be a disaster, if the flies were not carefully engineered to balance the weight with what's called a "counterweight system." The counterweight system makes sure that the weight of what is flying is carefully balanced at the other end of the rope. The **flyman** is the person in charge of pulling the ropes to make things go up and down, perfectly on cue—and gently so they don't crash. This takes a lot of practice, and since safety always comes first in the theater, a great deal of care goes into preparing lines for flying.

The other system of flying is by using machines called **winches**. These machines pull up and lower cable by winding and unwinding it, sort of like a giant fishing reel. The motor unspools letting more cable out and lowering the object. It can then reverse and wind the cable back onto the spool and raise the object. These motors are run by computers.

For Tarzan®, these actors had to learn to walk down a wall with a rope holding them up. It's harder than it looks!

DID YOU KNOW?

Sometimes stage flying is meant to be an illusion. In *Aida*, there was a set design for a swimming pool as seen from above. The audience saw the pool as if they were in the sky looking down at it, and it looked like two girls were swimming across the pool. In actuality, cables raised and lowered them into the air.

FLYING!

Every Disney show on Broadway flies its actors, but it's nothing new. In London in the late 1600's, "Restoration Spectaculars" were very elaborate stage productions that often had scenes of flying actors who arrived in the shows like angels with elaborate wings stuck to their backs and huge ropes attached to them from above.

When Mary Poppins flies up in the air with her famous umbrella, or when Peter Pan flies across the stage, the audience is meant to believe that it is some sort of magic that is lifting them up—even when we of course can see the wires. After all, nobody can *really* fly. And if they *can* fly, they certainly aren't wasting their time working in the theater!

Another kind of flying, or **aerial** work (aerial means "in the air") is used in *Tarzan*. In that show, the actors are like rock climbers, and they attach themselves to ropes or stretchy bungee cords to lift or bounce themselves up the walls. There is no attempt made to hide the wires. You are *supposed* to see them, just as you see the famous vine that all Tarzans swing on in the movies.

No matter whether it is meant to be an illusion, or intended that you see how it is done, all flying is pretty much the same—and a lot of fun to do. The actor wears a very secure (and often heavy) harness under his costume. It has special metal connectors that the cables attach to. Flying people in shows can be dangerous and requires a great deal of caution and many safety procedures, but it is always fun for the audience—especially when the actors fly right over them!

Argentinian aerial designer, Pichón Baldinu created all the flying effects for Tarzan®.

Stage Notes

★ *Peter Pan* is one of the most beloved stories in modern theater, but few people know that it also started a revolution in stage flying. In 1950, a young Englishman named Peter Foy sailed from London to New York to stage the flying for a Broadway play of *Peter Pan*. The show was so thrilling that the story was re-imagined as a musical just a few years later, and in 1954, Peter Foy famously returned to Broadway to fly Mary Martin as Peter Pan. Peter's company, Flying By Foy, became the standard of flying in the theater. Foy's flying systems have been used in *Beauty and the Beast*, *Aida*, *The Lion King*, *Tarzan*, and *Mary Poppins*.

★ Pichón Baldinu created the extraordinary flying moves in *Tarzan*, but he became famous for the ingenious theater company he cofounded in Argentina called De La Guarda. With this renegade theater company, he created some of the most imaginative stage flying ever seen. It was his approach with bungee cords and rock-climbing gear that caused *Tarzan* director Bob Crowley to ask him to create the flying and aerial gymnastics for *Tarzan*.

★ In the stage version of *Mary Poppins*, Bert the chimney sweep tap dances upside-down on the ceiling. The technique is the same as a "flying rig" but the result is something that has never happened on Broadway before!

When Ashley Brown flies as Mary Poppins, we try to disguise her wires (but, of course, you know they are there) for the illusion of flight.

In Tarzan® no one flies by "magic" so the flying ropes are completely visible throughout the performance, as shown here by Josh Strickland.

JOSH STRICKLAND

Sample swatches of gels (above) can make light many different colors.

AIDA SAND DUNE

AIDA SILK LINES

AIDA PALMS

The "gobos" create patterns of light onstage.

THE LIGHT STUFF

In Ancient Greece, live theater was performed in daylight, s... theaters were built in the open air and the lighting was take... care of by the sun. The ancient Romans came next, and they wer... probably the first to use torches and lamps for nighttime perfor... mances. Over a thousand years later, colored lights and fanc... ways to move the lighting around became part of the theater.

Most early lighting required some sort of fire, like oil lamps... candles, and torches to produce the special effects that audi... ences loved. They were also very dangerous, and back in thos... days theaters were constantly catching on fire. It's a good thing... the electric lightbulb was invented, because now, lighting is ... lot more fun and a lot less dangerous!

INSTRUMENTS, LAMPS, AND ELECTRICS: WHAT'S WHAT?

Everything we call *lighting* is part of the *electrics* department. The... thing that projects the light itself is called a lighting **instrument**...

Inside the lighting instrument is the **lamp**. The lamp in the... theater is what you call a lightbulb at home. What you call a lamp... at home, we call an instrument in the theater. Got it? Good... because that part always confuses me. Read it again and see i... you get it.

The next thing you need is something to control the colo... of the light. Most lights do this with some sort of color filter, o... what's called a **gel**, that the light passes through. (Think of these... as sort of like sunglasses for the lights.) As the beam of ligh... shoots out, the light turns whatever color the filter is. There are... many different types of color filters made of different materials...

You can also control the "shape" of the light by using ... **gobo**. A gobo is a thin circular plate with holes cut in it that... goes into the lighting instrument to create patterns... of projected light. Imagine if you took a piece of...

DID YOU KNOW?

There are enough lighting instruments in *Beauty and the Beast* to light up a football stadium!

oil, and cut a star shape out of it, and then put it over the end of a flashlight. When you point the flashlight at the wall, you'll see a star. That's what a gobo does.

Finally, you need some way to control all the instruments, so the lights come up or dim to a certain brightness at a certain speed. To do this you use a **lighting board**. Dimmers are part of the lighting board. They are just like the switches in your house that allow you to make the light brighter or dimmer. The exact same concept is used in the theater, except your mother isn't there yelling at you to "stop playing with those lights!"

WHAT ARE WE GOING TO LIGHT?

House Lights: **House lights** brighten the auditorium so the audience doesn't trip over each other or the seats. House lights can be very elaborate and beautiful, or they can be simple lights that can be turned on and off like a school classroom.

Traditional Lighting: There are two types of traditional lighting instruments: lights that **flood** or **wash** an area of the stage with light, and lights that illuminate very specific areas on the stage, or **spots**. These lights are positioned all around the theater, including "in the house" (facing the stage from the front), backstage (facing toward the stage), or even above the stage, pointing down.

Moving Lights: It used to be that lights were positioned and locked down with clamps to point at just one area. Today, there are lights that have motors inside them that move all by themselves without anyone there to guide them. A computer sends a signal to the light and it moves to a preprogrammed location. When you see lots of beams of light sweeping the stage at the same time, you know you are seeing computerized **moving lights**.

Follow Spots: **Follow spots** are lighting instruments that work like very bright, gigantic flashlights. An operator controls the light, aims it at a specific actor, and follows him wherever he goes. Follow spots are useful to make sure that an actor never steps into a dark area, and also to make clear to the audience who the star is by keeping him in the brightest light no matter where he goes.

Natasha Katz has designed lights for Beauty and the Beast, Aida, On the Record, Tarzan®, *and* The Little Mermaid. *We like her a lot.*

Produced by Walt Disney Theatrical Productions, Ltd.		
Directed by: Robert Falls	Set by: Bob Crowley	
LIGHTING BY: NATASHA KATZ		
Drawing: LIGHT PLOT	Associate Designer: Dan Walker	
Scale: 1/4" = 1'-0"	Drawing # 2 of 6	Date: 11/15/01	Revised:
	Drawn by: DW	

L. D. 170
LIGHTING DESIGNER
SIGNATURE

105

Look how different these three scenes from The Little Mermaid look, all because of lighting.

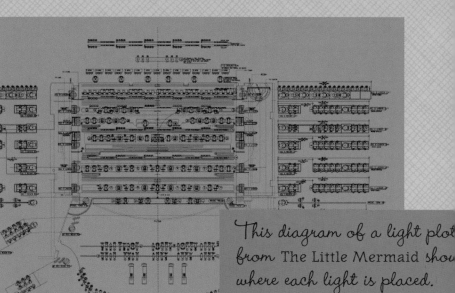

This diagram of a light plot from The Little Mermaid shows where each light is placed.

Ghost Light: The **ghost light** is a single light bulb that stands glowing on the stage in every empty theater. The last thing you do in the theater before locking up at night is put the ghost light downstage center and turn it on.

Despite its mysterious name, this light is a safety device to make sure that a theater, with all its dangers, is never left in the dark. If there weren't a ghost light, the first guy who arrived in the morning would stand a good chance of falling through a trapdoor or stumbling into the open orchestra pit. Then he just might *become* a ghost!

When you think about lighting, you think about lighting the stage and what's on it like people, scenery, props or even the floor. But have you ever thought about lighting the air? Lighting designers frequently use a sort of fog or smoke effect on stage. When they shine beams of lights though smoke they can create patterns or color in the air. Best not to try this at home!

LIMELIGHT

No one uses limelight anymore, but the expression "to be in the limelight" still refers to when someone is in the public's eye. The expression comes from when actors used to be very visible onstage while standing in the limelight.

Lime is a powder that, when heated by a flame, glows brightly without ever catching on fire. If you put a reflector behind it, the glowing lime casts light onto the stage. Lime was popular before the invention of electric lighting, and was yet another reason theaters were always burning down. The lime may not have caught fire when heated—but everything around it did!

You might be wondering why keeping fire *out* of the theater was such a hard idea to grasp in the old days. The answer is simple. Fire was used to create beauty onstage, and no one who has ever made theater is willing to compromise what they think will make the show great. Even if it means burning the place down!

The ghost light protects the theater and everyone in it.

The prop vase in Mary Poppins breaks just the same each time—before it's put back together for the next show.

Props

A **prop** is any object held, manipulated, or carried by a performer during a theatrical performance. It is short for "property." If someone grabbed your bag and took your stuff you might say, "Hey! Leave that alone! It is my property." Well in the theater everything that isn't scenery or costumes is a property, or prop. A vase of flowers is a prop. A cane is a prop. A bottle of cola is a prop. It doesn't need to be the real thing, and in fact, the real thing often doesn't work as well as a fake. What's important is how it looks, or "reads," from out front. Props can even look silly close-up, but what matters is how they look to the audience.

There are lots of tricks to props. They often are specially designed to create an effect—like a bag of groceries that breaks open at the bottom just as an actress walks in the door, or a vase like one in *Mary Poppins* that falls and smashes every night and then gets put back together backstage to smash again the next night. The trick vase, plus a great sound effect, makes the audience believe it is real and that it is really breaking.

Prop food is always interesting. Eating onstage is difficult to do because you need to keep talking, and on top of that many actors are very fussy about what they eat and when. As much as possible, actors try to pretend they are eating when they can get away with it. If they do have to eat, the prop department sorts exactly what it will be and how it will look and taste. It is best not to get your hopes up about how it will taste.

Props also need to be carefully organized backstage. Nothing is worse than not being able to find your prop before you run onstage. There are legendary stories in the theater about props that don't work or go missing during the show. Nothing is worse at the time it happens, and nothing is funnier a few years later.

PROPERTY MASTER

The **property master** creates, finds, organizes, and manages the props for the show. It is a very complicated job and on some shows requires the work of several people in the department. Some shows are very prop-oriented, like *Mary Poppins*, with lots of tricks and tools and small items everywhere. Prop master Victor Amerling has a big job for that show!

Stage Notes

★ The realistic-looking wooden prop furniture that decorates a tent in *Tarzan* is all made out of soft foam rubber, so that the actors playing apes won't hurt themselves when they smash it all up in the song "Trashin' the Camp."

★ There are three prop dogs in *Mary Poppins* that look so realistic some people have asked how we trained the dog to be so still on-stage. They were actually made by the same man who made the original costume for the popular star of the TV show *Bear In the Big Blue House*.

★ The elephant that nightly walks down the aisle in *The Lion King* on Broadway is a prop that takes four actors inside it to make the journey. After it gets to the stage and makes its exit, it is stored for the rest of the show fifteen feet up in the air over the stage. It is too big to fit anywhere else.

★ The character of Belle's father, Maurice, in *Beauty and the Beast* makes an invention that chops wood and drives around the stage. On Broadway, this prop has traveled more than 340,000 feet. That's nearly 65 miles!

ANN ARVIA

A rubber typewriter, a talking dog, even something as basic as a basketball are all called props on stage.

JOHN TARTAGLIA

Special Effects

Special effects aren't the sole responsibility of any single depart ment. Some special effects are part of the props department Others are part of lighting. Some are part of the costumes **Special effects** are visual elements such as fog, smoke, light ning, breaking furniture, snow, or the like, that require specia tricks to effect reality or fantasy on the stage.

PYROTECHNICS

The illusion of fire and explosions is known in the theater a **pyrotechnics**, or "pyro" for short. Many shows have pyro ef fects. When *Beauty and the Beast* first opened on Broadway every night the champagne bottles in the "Be Our Guest" numbe exploded with flying sparks at the end of the song, sort of lik something you would see on the Fourth of July. That was a pyr

DID YOU KNOW?

When the idea of putting *Beauty and the Beast* onstage was just starting to form, one of the problems everyone thought about was how they would make a "human" candlestick walk around on stage? Everyone knows the character of Lumiere from the animated movie, but those flames were drawings. Onstage it takes special technology, and in the last twelve years, it has taken 574 pounds of butane to light his hands. That's a lot of pyro!

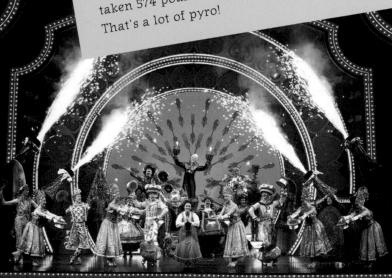

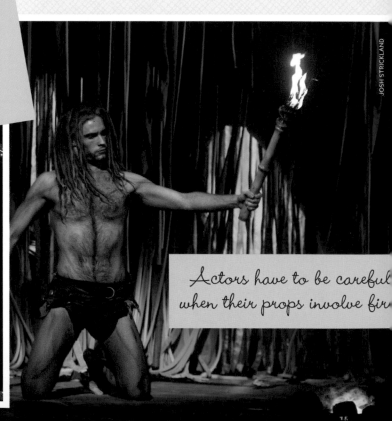

JOSH STRICKLAND

Actors have to be careful when their props involve fir

effect. The character Tarzan makes a fire and then lights a torch in one of the scenes to find his way in the dark. That effect is also pyro. Mary Poppins claps her hands and makes a nasty lady disappear into a cloud of smoke that pops up out of the floor. That smoke effect is also a pyrotechnic effect.

For as long as the theater has been around, flashes of fire and smoke have been used onstage to create a dynamic effect and to thrill audiences.

MAGIC AND ILLUSION

Sometimes you need to perform magic tricks onstage. In the case of some Disney shows, this is required to give the impression that something impossible has been achieved, almost as if the performer had magic or supernatural powers. Everyone knows that Mary Poppins has special powers. Everything she owns, including a potted plant, a hat rack, a mirror, her bed, her books, and all of her clothes, fits into a small carpetbag that she carries into the nursery. How does it all fit in there? It fits by magic, or *stage illusion*. I'm sure you'd love to know how those kind of stage illusions are created, but a good magician never gives away his tricks! You'll just have to work in the theater to find out how it's done!

Magicians train a lifetime to perform "tricks," but actors onstage need to learn them quickly, and directors need to figure out how to make those tricks happen. That's when you call in a specialist to create the illusions for the show.

Mary Poppins uses stage magic to pull many things out of her carpetbag, including a four-foot-tall potted palm!

JOHN TIGGELOVEN

Being a good technical director requires a lot of experience and a very cool head.

Putting It All Together

TECHNICAL DIRECTOR

The **technical director** is responsible for the delivery and operation of all technical aspects of the production. It is a challenging and exciting job. Of course, like many aspects of the theater, if everything goes brilliantly, very few people notice what a good job the tech director did. If the scenery crumbles to the floor everyone *blames* the tech director.

Technical directors have to know about all aspects of backstage life, from carpentry, to electrics, to props, to automated scenery, to *you name it*. If it is onstage and it doesn't have a heartbeat, it is the responsibility of the technical director. Technical directors come to the job from many different areas of the theater, but the great ones like John Tiggeloven (known throughout the theater simply as "Tigg") take on the job because they love to see things run well. The satisfaction of solving problems and making things run smoothly fuels the best guys in the business.

STAGE MANAGEMENT TEAM

Stage managers are the lifeblood of rehearsing, running, and maintaining a show. They are in charge of the rehearsal room and call each rehearsal to order. They work with the director to plan the rehearsal process and are responsible for making the rehearsal room look, feel, and operate as though the actual show were taking place.

Stage managers maintain the script and integrate all new scenes and songs into it. They also balance between the technical and artistic worlds. The stage manager learns the show intimately and, with the director, creates the "flow" of the production. It is one of the stage managers who, during each rehearsal, follows the prompt script and "calls the cues" for the lights and scene changes. Everyone in the theater waits for the stage manager to say "go!" before they execute the next lighting cue or scenic change. In a song called "Step In Time" from *Mary Poppins*, cues come fast and furious, and the stage manager is in constant verbal contact with the crew onstage

Take a look at this page from the prompt script to see how many "cues" stage manager Theresa Bailey calls during this scene in The Little Mermaid.

and out front to make it all happen. She wears a headset so she can hear everything the crew needs to tell her, and she has a microphone to talk to each of them. During the song, the lights are changing, follow spots are following, chimneys are moving right and left, and a man is walking upside down on the ceiling—all under the control of the stage manager, who calls cues every second of the song. On a big show, the stage manager has a series of TV monitors showing all different angles of the stage and the wings to make sure every*one* and every*thing* is in place before they say GO!

Every show is different, and each stage manager and stage management team divides up the job differently, but from the time everyone walks through

WHAT'S MY CUE?

A cue is a prompt that the stage manager gives to someone so that they do something at the right moment. There are several types of cues. Light cues are the various changes the board operator makes to the lights. If there are 248 light cues in the show, the lighting changes that many times. There can be a cue for a piece of scenery to move to a different place between scene changes. There are also cues for actors. The director might say, "Your cue to enter is when you hear the gun go off." If the gun doesn't actually go off, things get a little out of whack, so cues are important because they keep things moving smoothly. When there's no other way to communicate with the person who's supposed to do something, the stage manager will use "cue lights," which are little lights that go on to signal a cue.

113

the stage door to the final curtain, the stage manager is i charge of the production. It is her job to keep the pace o the cues, to protect the actors and the crew, to be mindfu of problems that might be ahead, and to solve problems a they come up.

If you want to know what's going on in a theater, as the stage manager. Many directors and producers began thei careers as stage managers. It is one of the few areas tha touch almost every aspect of the production, from script and design, to actors, wardrobe, makeup, wigs, and lighting. Stag managers are generally not responsible for anything "out in the house" meaning anything dealing with the public. They don' work with ushers, ticket takers, the box office, or press and marketing—but if it is backstage, a good stage manager is a over it!

STAGE CREW

There are three key stage-crew departments that run what hap pens on the stage (in addition to wardrobe, which we discussed earlier). Each of these departments has a "head" of the depart ment, known on Broadway as house heads. If you have grea house heads, you are a lucky producer.

The stage-crew departments are:

Electrics: This team manages everything that has electricity running to it. They are responsible, of course, for running the lighting, maintaining the lighting instruments and the lighting board, and also all of the sound equipment. The lighting board operator, the soundboard operator, the follow-spot operators and all electricians on the deck are part of the electrics de partment. When the stage gets smoky to create a cool lighting effect, it's the electrics department running the machine tha makes the smoke and light. If it lights up, turns on, or has a switch, it is probably part of "electrics."

Props: The props department manages the props and also sets the props up whether they are pre-set in the wing or put onstage before the curtain goes up. The props de partment works with the set designer to create the prop nd maintain them for the run of e show. If you pick it up, eat , hit someone with it, shoot it, wing it, carry it, or toss it, the rop department is responsible or it. They are also responsible or maintaining a clean stage floor nd for miscellaneous furniture ackstage, like chairs and tables. eople in the prop department are xceptionally handy. Everyone ould like a good prop person at ome to help around the house.

arpentry: At home, carpenters uild stuff out of wood, but in the heater the carpentry department ncludes the people who manage e big stuff. They are in charge f the scenery and the machines hat make the scenery move around the tage. If it flies onto the stage, carpentry responsible for what is flying (even if is a person), as well as the thing that akes it fly. The carpentry department is esponsible for elevators and of course he scenery on the elevators. Trap doors nd the entire deck itself belong to the arpentry department. If you can fall nto it, or fall from it, or fall through it, he carpentry department is probably esponsible for it.

The crew has to be very careful with the glasslike scenery in The Little Mermaid.

Victor Amerling, head of the prop department, sweeps up the flower petals that he showers onto the Mary Poppins set every night.

Jeff Goodman is the head carpen- ter on Tarzan®. How can you be a carpenter on a set that's inflated?

Stage Notes

STAGE SUPERSTITIONS

Superstitions have always played a large role in the theater. Maybe it's because it is so hard to tell why shows are successful; maybe because it's so scary to go out there and perform; or maybe it's because theaters are like old houses with lots of history, ghosts, and spirits in them. Superstitions can be anything from not wanting to say the last line of a play before the first audience comes, to not wanting to rehearse the curtain call before the final rehearsal, to wearing a pair of "lucky socks" on opening night. No matter what an actor's superstition may be, NEVER tell a superstitious actor he's crazy. He already knows that. He became an actor!

Here are a couple of famous stage superstitions:

★ **Mac-Shuuush!**
Shakespeare's famous tragedy *Macbeth* is said to be cursed, and to avoid problems actors never say the title of the play out loud when inside a theater or a theatrical space (like a rehearsal room or costume or scene shop). Since the play is set in Scotland, the secret code you say when you need to say the title of the play is "the Scottish play." If you do say the title by accident, legend has it you have to go outside, turn around three times, and come back into the theater. Just don't say it, and you'll be fine.

★ **Breaking a Leg is Good?**
In the theater it is considered bad luck to wish people "good luck." So if you want to wish someone good luck in the theater, you have to wish them bad luck instead by saying, "break a leg." The idea is that no matter what you say, the fates will turn against it, so if you wish bad luck, it'll turn to good! Frankly, most people don't know why they say it, but everyone says, "break a leg" before a show, and no one says, "good luck." Ever. If you think that's crazy, many French performers whisper a dirty word for "poop" in your ear and then kiss you on the cheek before you go onstage.

Lucky socks?

ENCORE Stuff That Will Be Useful After You Finish Reading This Book

Putting On a Play

There are many ways to put on a play at home or at school. Yo can set your garage or your classroom up, write a play of yo own, and invite your friends or other students to get involve All you need is a story to tell.

There are also many plays that have already been writter and those are fun to produce and act in as well. One of th best places to go to learn about these shows is Music The atre International. When I was starting in the theater, I wou spend hours reading the catalogs of the plays that my frienc and I wanted to put on. Now, many of those plays are at Musi Theatre International, and you can put on your own version c *Aladdin, Jungle Book, Mulan, High School Musical,* or eve *Beauty and the Beast.*

You can get the scripts and the music and even suggestior for how to stage it. Ask someone you know to help you loc at their Web site. Lots c Disney shows are there, a well as other great musical such as *Annie, The Musr Man,* and *West Side Stor* These are the shows I pe formed in growing up, and had a ball.

Don't Forget Your Theater-Speak!

Book The script of a musical show.

Cast The group of performers that appear in a show. To "cast" a show is to pick the actors.

Closing Notice A dreadful sign that goes up to tell everyone that a play is closing in two weeks—which is the official amount of notice you must give actors. If you close with only one night's notice, you still have to pay them for two weeks.

Curtain Call The end of a show, when the cast bows in front of an audience that is clapping really loud and screaming "Bravo!" Well, they don't always scream, but you do hope they clap.

Five Minutes An announcement the stage manager makes to tell actors they have five minutes before getting to the stage for the first scene. Backstage you would hear, "Five minutes, ladies and gentlemen. Five minutes to places. This is your five-minute call." Sometimes just hearing those words really makes your heart race.

Hit A very successful show. The opposite of a hit show is a flop. Nobody wants to produce a flop, but it happens.

House Seats Seats reserved for the producer and theater owner, so that their friends get good seats whenever they call. I get lots of calls for my house seats.

Lines Generally, in the theater lines are the words actors say onstage. Actors often ask, "What's my first line in this scene?" or "When do I say that line?" Some actors count their lines to see if they have a good part. Smart actors are happy to have a part that is interesting whether they say a lot or not.

Melody The part of a song that's just the music. For example, sing "Twinkle, Twinkle, Little Star." That's a song. Now hum it without the words. That is the melody of the song.

Open-ended Run A show that will keep performing until people stop coming. The opposite of an open-ended run is a "limited engagement." That's when there are a fixed number of performances planned from the very beginning.

Places The stage manager says "places" to tell actors when to go to the stage and prepare for the curtain to go up.

Running Time How long the play takes to perform, including intermission. You might ask the house manager or box office person what the running time is so you can arrange for a ride home after the show.

Set The objects on stage when the actors are performing. A set can be elaborate and realistic, like a fancy house, or it can be a bunch of blue silk to make you think the play is happening in the sky, or a set might be just a chair and a table.

Standing Ovation When the audience is so excited about what they saw that clapping just isn't enough, they often stand and clap. Everyone likes to get a standing ovation.

For More Information...

Your local library is a treasure trove of more great books about the theater. I love spending time with theater books. Maybe you'll find some of these next time you go book hunting.

BOOKS

For Adults and Young Adults

The McGraw-Hill Theatergoer's Guide by Edwin Wilson. McGraw-Hill, 2001.
The Theater Experience by Edwin Wilson. McGraw-Hill, 2001.

Teaching Books for Adults

Kids Take the Stage by Lenka Peterson and Dan O'Connor. Backstage Books, 1997.
On Stage: Theater Games and Activities for Kids by Lisa Bany-Winters. Chicago Review Press, 1997.

Acting and Performance

101 Drama Games for Children: Fun and Learning with Acting and Make-Believe by Paul Rooyackers, illustrated by Cecilia Bowman. Hunter House, 1
Acting & Theatre (An Usborne Introduction), by Cheryl Evans and Lucy Smith. E.D.C. Publishing, 1992.
Break a Leg!: The Kids' Guide to Acting and Stagecraft by Lise Friedman. Workman Publishing, 2002.

For Young Readers

Acting A to Z: The Young Person's Guide to a Stage or Screen Career by Katherine Mayfield. Backstage Books, 1998.
Bravo! Brava! A Night at the Opera: Behind the Scenes with Composers, Cast, and Crew by Anne Siberell. Oxford University Press, 2001.
Pamela's First Musical by Wendy Wasserstein, illustrated by Andrew Jackness. Hyperion, 1998.
The Great American Mousical by Julie Andrews Edwards and Emma Walton Hamilton, illustrated by Tony Walton. HarperCollins, 2006.
Welcome to the Globe! The Story of Shakespeare's Theater by Peter Chrisp. Dorling Kindersley, 2000.

WEB SITES

How Does the Show Go On?
www.howdoestheshowgoon.com

Disney on Broadway
www.disneyonbroadway.com

Educational Theatre Association—International Thespian Society / Dramatics Magazine
www.edta.org

Music Theatre International—Broadway Junior and MTI's KIDS Collections
www.mtishows.com

Rosie's Broadway Kids
www.rosiesbroadwaykids.com

TheaterMania's Theater for Kids
www.theatermania.com/kids

Afterword

Writing a book about the theater for people just learning about it is more fun than I ever expected. I love working in the theater, and even though it is awful when critics don't like what I've done and I go for long periods without seeing my family and friends, I've never felt more at home anyplace else.

In the theater, you are always learning. I've asked many of my theater friends to check over sections of this book and they often say, "Hey I didn't know that." It seems all of us have a lot to learn about our chosen craft. I know I still do.

Teachers have immeasurably enriched my life, and there is no one I'm more grateful for every time I enter a theater than the wonderful people who were and are my teachers, whether in school, in life, or in theater. Four of them come to mind from when I was younger. Marian Haworth took me under her wing, taught me about technical theater, and put me to work as a volunteer hanging lights, building scenery, and working on stage crews when I was fourteen years old. To this day, I use much of what she taught me. Roy Casstevens taught me about directing and producing and dreams from the time I was fifteen, and not a day goes by that I don't use some aspect of what I learned from him. Berle Davis was my dance teacher when I was fifteen until I was eighteen, and everything I know about discipline, practice, and respect in the theater goes back to Berle. Finally, John Cauble at UCLA taught me what producing was all about and set me on a path to become what I am today.

If you have great teachers, listen to them. If you have a chance to be a teacher to someone, somewhere, somehow, be one. And in the theater, never forget that you will always be a student.

Photo Credits

Page 2: Gino Domenico
Page 5: Michael Carroll
Page 6 (bottom): Lindsay Jones
Page 7: Illustration by Scott Tilley
Page 10: Whitney Cox Photography
Page 11 (left and center): Joan Marcus
Page 11 (right): © iStockphoto.com/byphoto
Page 12 (top): © iStockphoto.com/Murdo
Page 12 (center): Joan Marcus
Page 12 (bottom): David Crosswaite
Page 13 (top): Alan Ross Kosher
Page 13 (bottom left): Michael Cassel
Page 13 (bottom right): Pat Switzer
Page 14 (top): Courtesy of Center Theatre Group/ Mark Taper Forum
Page 14 (center): mollie boice
Page 14 (bottom): Danielle Santana
Page 15 (right): Randall Michelson
Page 15 (inset): Jane Hoffer/Courtesy of Lincoln Center Institute for the Arts in Education
Page 16–17: Illustrations by Scott Tilley
Page 17 (bottom left): © iStockphoto.com/Liliboas
Page 18–19: Lyn Hughes
Page 20 (left): Lyn Hughes
Page 20 (bottom center and bottom right): Joan Marcus
Page 21 (top): Ed Kreiger
Page 21 (center and bottom): Gino Domenico
Page 22: Gino Domenico
Page 23: Gino Domenico
Page 24: Gino Domenico
Page 25 (top, center, and bottom): Gino Domenico
Page 26: Gino Domenico
Page 28 (Playbills): From PLAYBILL. Copyright © 1994, 2000, 2005, and 2006. Reprinted by permission of Playbill, Inc.
Page 28 (Playbill insert): From STAGEBILL. Copyright © 1997. Reprinted by permission of Playbill, Inc.
Page 29 (top): Whitney Cox Photography
Page 29 (bottom): Joan Marcus
Page 30: Joan Marcus
Page 31 (top and bottom left): Joan Marcus
Page 31 (bottom right): Gino Domenico
Page 32 (top): Frank Veronsky
Page 32 (center and bottom): Joan Marcus
Page 33: Joan Marcus
Page 34 (left): 2006 Bruce Glikas
Page 34 (bottom left): © iStockphoto.com/nickfree
Page 34 (bottom right): Dave Cross
Page 35: Tony Russell
Page 36 (top): Joan Marcus
Page 36 (bottom left): © iStockphoto.com/cveltri
Page 36 (bottom right): Gerard Barnier
Page 37: Joan Marcus
Page 38 (top): Anita & Steve Shevett © 1998
Page 38 (center): Joan Marcus
Page 38 (bottom): 2006 Bruce Glikas

Page 39 (top): Joan Marcus
Page 39 (bottom): Dusty Bennett
Page 40 (top and center): Joan Marcus
Page 40 (bottom): © iStockphoto.com/inkit
Page 41: 2006 Bruce Glikas
Page 42 (top): Joan Marcus
Page 42 (center): Basil Childers
Page 42 (bottom left): Mark van der Zouw
Page 42 (bottom right): © iStockphoto.com/dugpark
Page 43 (top and bottom): Joan Marcus
Page 43 (center): Kenneth Van Sickle
Page 44: Joan Marcus
Page 45: Joan Marcus
Page 46 (top): Joan Marcus
Page 46 (center): 2007 Bruce Glikas
Page 47: Joan Marcus
Page 48: Michael Le Poer Trench
Page 49 (photo and inset): Joan Marcus
Page 50 (left, top to bottom): Dusty Bennett
Page 50 (right, top): Gino Domenico
Page 50 (right, bottom): Dusty Bennett
Page 52 (photo 2 and 3): Kenneth Van Sickle
Page 53 (photo 4): Joan Marcus
Page 54: Joan Marcus
Page 55: Gino Domenico
Page 56 (top and bottom): Joan Marcus
Page 57: Dusty Bennett
Page 58 (top): Portrait by Ruven Afanador
Page 58 (bottom left): Rendering by Bob Crowley
Page 58 (bottom right): Joan Marcus
Page 58 (portfolio): Renderings by Julie Taymor
Page 59: Joan Marcus
Page 60 (top, center, and bottom right): Joan Marcus
Page 60 (bottom left): © iStockphoto.com/EuToch
Page 61: Per Breiehagen
Page 62 (top left feature photos and bottom right feature photos): Gino Domenico.
Page 62 (top right): Joan Marcus
Page 62 (bottom left): © iStockphoto.com/jld0476
Page 63: Mark van der Zouw
Page 64: Joan Marcus
Page 65 (bottom left): © iStockphoto.com/selensergen
Page 65 (bottom center and right): Joan Marcus
Page 66: Joan Marcus
Page 67 (background): Joan Marcus
Page 67 (feature photos): Gino Domenico
Page 67 (left and right): Per Breiehagen
Page 69 (top): Per Breiehagen
Page 69 (center and bottom): Joan Marcus
Page 70: Per Breiehagen
Page 71: Dusty Bennett
Page 72–73: Joan Marcus
Page 74–75: Joan Marcus
Page 76: Gino Domenico
Page 76 (diagram): Courtesy of Aubrey Lynch II
Page 78 (top): Joan Marcus
Page 78 (bottom): Patrick Goodwin
Page 79: Joan Marcus
Page 80 (top and bottom): Joan Marcus
Page 81: Joan Marcus

Page 82 (top and bottom): Joan Marcus
Page 83 (top and bottom): Joan Marcus
Page 84: Joan Marcus
Page 85 (left): Joan Marcus
Page 85 (right): Per Breiehagen
Page 86 (top and bottom): Michael Carroll
Page 87 (top and center): Michael Carroll
Page 87 (bottom): Joan Marcus
Page 88: Gino Domenico
Page 89 (top and bottom): Joan Marcus
Page 90: © iStockphoto.com/sdourado
Page 91 (background): © iStockphoto.com/Cimmerian
Page 91 (inset): Rendering by Kenneth Foy
Page 92 (top, center, and bottom): Joan Marcus
Page 93: Joan Marcus
Page 94 (left and inset): Joan Marcus
Page 95 (top): Gino Domenico
Page 95 (center and bottom): Dusty Bennett
Page 96 (top): Crosby Clyse
Page 96 (center): Dusty Bennett
Page 96 (bottom): Gino Domenico
Page 97 (top, bottom left, and bottom right): Joan Marcus
Page 98 (top and center): Joan Marcus
Page 98 (bottom): Kenneth Van Sickle
Page 99 (background): Gino Domenico
Page 99 (left and right): Joan Marcus
Page 100: Joan Marcus
Page 101: Joan Marcus
Page 102 (background and inset): Joan Marcus
Page 103 (background and inset): Joan Marcus
Page 104 (top): Joan Marcus
Page 104 (center): Courtesy of NK Productions, Inc.
Page 104 (bottom): George Holz
Page 105: Thomas Schumacher
Page 106 (top left, top right, and bottom left): Joan Marcus
Page 106 (bottom right): Courtesy of NK Productions, Inc.
Page 107 (top): Joan Marcus
Page 107 (bottom): Dusty Bennett
Page 108 (top, center, and bottom): Joan Marcus
Page 109 (top): Dusty Bennett
Page 109 (center and bottom): Joan Marcus
Page 110 (top, bottom left, and bottom right): Joan Marcus
Page 111 (feature photos): Joan Marcus
Page 112 (background): Rob Halliday
Page 112 (inset): Dusty Bennett
Page 113: Crosby Clyse
Page 115 (top and bottom): Joan Marcus
Page 115 (center): Dusty Bennett
Page 116: © iStockphoto.com/aheinzen
Page 117: Yvette Marie Dostatni
Page 118 (top): Copyright, Pittsburgh Post-Gazette, 2007, all rights reserved. Reprinted with Permission
Page 118 (bottom): Linda Federico-O'Murchú
Page 119: Arnold Morascher
Page 124: Illustration by Scott Tilley
Page 126–127: From PLAYBILL. Copyright © 1994, 1997, 2000, 2004, and 2006. Reprinted by permission of Playbill, Inc.
Page 128: Gino Domenico

Acknowledgments

...e list of people who appear in this book and helped along the way is deep. We are grateful to each and every one of them.

...ramount to acknowledge is Dusty, Dusty, and Dusty. And then I need to make sure I thank. . . who is it? Oh, yes, Dusty.

...endy for endless permission, support, guidance and intelligence, Jenna, Meghan, and Kasey for doing the darn thing, and ...beautifully, Matthew for nurturing, and supporting, and tolerating.

...ost of all, my thanks goes to Jeff Kurtti who for twenty-three years has provided endless repartee, boundless encour-...ement, a whack on the head with a rolled-up newspaper when required, and the words that made this book possible, ...When do we start?"

...addition, this book wouldn't have happened without the cooperation and support of the following people:

...ana Amendola, Jane Austin, Peter Avery, Edwin Belen, Chris Berger, Phil Birsh, Cynthia Boardman, Jim Boese, Steve ...orell, Roy Casstevens, Eduardo Castro, Ken Cerniglia, Stephanie Cheek, Crosby Clyse, Keith Cooper, Stephen Crocker, ...auren Daghini, Mark Dobrow, Naomi Donne, Steven Downing, Dave Ehle, Laura Eichholz, Jack Eldon, Steve Fickinger, Cristi ...nn, Allan Frost, Harry Gold, Denise J. Grillo, Dayle Gruet, Juliana Hannett, Gregory Hanoian, Jonathan Hanson, Michael ...eight, Scott Hemerling, Nancy Hereford, Joel Hile, Jane Hodges, Victor Irving, Robbin Kelley, Sean Kenny, Bit Knighton, ...ric Kratzer, Vanessa Kromer, Rick Kunis, Carl Lembo, Johanna Lester, Hans Ligtvoet, John Loiacono, Frank Lombardi, Frank ...ott, Shaina Low, Aubrey Lynch, Jimmy Maloney, Joan Marcus, Carlos Martinez, Gary Martori, Joe McClafferty, Angus ...cIndoe, Aaron Meier, Jan Meiselman, Randy Meyer, Roger Michelson, Cara Moccia, Melanie Montes, Alex Near, Jonathan ...lson, Kelli Palan, Francesca Panagopoulos, Janine Paver, Tim Pettolina, Matt Polk, Anne Quart, Julie Ratcliffe, Kendra ...eid, Mark Rozzano, Nick Scandalios, Thomas Schlenk, Clifford Schwartz, David Scott, Benjy Shaw, Deborah Shrimpton, ...rew Siccardi, Seth Stuhl, Richard Swan, Susanne Tighe, Dana Torres, Jason Trubitt, Sjoerd van Schooten, Ron Vodicka, ...essie Ward, Ann Wareham, Kyle Wilson, Martin Wiviott, Doc Zorthian, and Frank Zwolinsky.

About the Authors

Thomas Schumacher

Thomas Schumacher was born in California sometime during the last century. Before computers or fax machines. Befo[...] video games or color television. Before CDs and DVDs —but after Ethel Merman opened in *Gypsy*. That's all anyone nee[...] to know about that.

Like all kids who can read well out loud, he thought he was an actor. It turned out he wasn't much of an actor, but his lo[...] for theater led him to do everything else backstage and in the front of house.

He has made his living at one time or another as a shoe salesman, costume dyer, actor, gift wrapper, director, bus bc[...] production assistant, kitchen worker, box-office treasurer, custodian, film executive, driver, teacher, puppeteer, mov[...] producer, playground leader, stage carpenter, sound operator, sandwich maker, stage manager, personal assistant to a famo[...] actress, and most recently, as a Broadway producer.

On Broadway for Disney, he has produced *King David, The Lion King, Elton John* and *Tim Rice's Aida, Tarzan* with mus[...] by Phil Collins, and *Mary Poppins* with Cameron Mackintosh. On tour, he produced *On The Record,* a collection of Disne[...] songs, as well as a stage version of *The Hunchback of Notre Dame* in Berlin, Germany. His shows have been seen outsic[...] of Broadway in major cities like London, Toronto, Hamburg, Amsterdam, Tokyo, Seoul, Sydney, Melbourne, Shanghai, ar[...] on various tours throughout the United States and abroad.

Also for Disney, he produced the animated film *The Rescuers Down Under* and was executive producer of the film *Th[...] Lion King*. For Disney animation he also supervised the development and production of some twenty feature films, includir[...] *Mulan, Lilo and Stitch, Pocahontas, Tarzan®,* and *Tim Burton's The Nightmare Before Christmas.*

Before all of that, he worked for a ballet company, did everything anyone asked at the Mark Taper Forum, was a staff producer on the 1984 Olympic Arts Festival, and brought *Cirque du Soleil* to America for the very first time as part of the Los Angeles Festival. He went to school at the University of California, Los Angeles, where he studied theater and dreamed of getting to do it for a living.

He lives in New York.

Jeff Kurtti

Jeff Kurtti was born in Seattle, Washington, and from day one, it seemed, was destined to work with Disney. Jeff, too, thought he was an actor, but when he grew up and stopped being cute and precocious, acting was out—but he still followed the Disney path.

Over the years, he has worked as a movie-theater usher, a publicist, a graphic artist, personal assistant to an arts executive, a Walt Disney Imagineer, and a Walt Disney Company marketing rep. Soon he found that he could write books about the things he liked, and other people would be interested and pay him to do it!

He is the author of books like *The Great Movie Musical Trivia Book; The Art of Mulan; A Bug's Life: The Making of an Epic of Miniature Proportions; Since the World Began: Walt Disney World—The First 25 Years; The Art of Disneyland;* and *Disney Dossiers.*

Jeff also took a stab at making video productions, and got to work on DVD collector's editions of great movies like *Around the World in 80 Days; The Adventures of Robin Hood; The Lord of the Rings: The Fellowship of the Ring; Tarzan; Toy Story; Fantasia; Snow White and the Seven Dwarfs; Beauty and the Beast;* and a large portion of the Walt Disney Treasures DVD edition series with Leonard Maltin.

For a time, he did everything anyone asked him to at the Paramount Theater and the Fifth Avenue Theater in Seattle before moving to Los Angeles, where he worked on the 1984 Olympic Arts Festival. It was there that he met a young staff producer who became a lasting and loyal friend and supporter, and an all-around fun and favorite guy—Thomas Schumacher.

Jeff currently lives in Glendale, California, with three of his other fun and favorite guys: Kenneth, Brendan, and Baby Joseph.

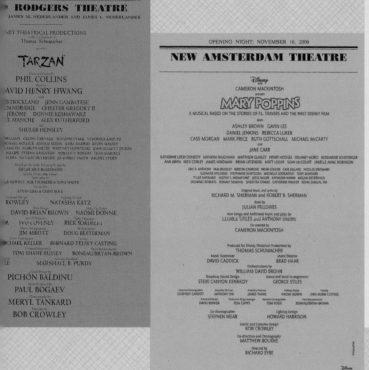

RICHARD
RODGERS
THEATRE
226 WEST 46th ST.
STAGE DOOR

The End